Food of Scotland

Excerpted from *The Taste of Britain*

Laura Mason and Catherine Brown

EXCLUSIVE EDITION FOR

THE SCOTSMAN

Harper*Press*
An Imprint of HarperCollinsPublishers

Harper*Press*
An imprint of HarperCollins Publishers
77–85 Fulham Palace Road,
Hammersmith, London W6 8JB
www.harpercollins.co.uk

Published by Harper Press in 2006

This edition produced especially for *The Scotsman*

First published in Great Britain in 1999
as *Traditional Foods of Britain*
by Prospect Books
Allaleigh House, Blackawton, Totnes, Devon TQ9 7DL

A catalogue record for this book
is available from the British Library

ISBN-13 978-0-00-778524-7
ISBN-10 0-00-778524-0

Typeset by Davidson Pre-Press, Glasgow

Printed and bound in Great Britain

Contents

South Scotland: East, South, Central & Borders

Arbroath Smokie

DESCRIPTION:

A HOT-SMOKED, HEADED, GUTTED, UNFILLETED HADDOCK. WEIGHT: 250G–300G. COLOUR: COPPER-BROWN ON OUTSIDE, FLESH INSIDE CREAMY WHITE. FLAVOUR: MELLOW OVERTONES OF SALT AND SMOKE.

HISTORY:

First developed in Auchmithie, a fishing village a little north of Arbroath, this was originally known as an Auchmithie lucken or close fish or pinwiddie. Auchmithie was largely populated by families of Norse origin. Their names still bear the evidence. The Norse-descended Spink family owns the largest traditional smokie-curing company in Arbroath. Auchmithie was also un-usual amongst other fishing villages of that coast in its setting of the fisher-houses high on the edge of a cliff above the harbour several hundred feet below.

The fish were originally smoked over domestic fires, but the need for more smoking facilities caused numerous 'smoke-pits' to be set up in half whisky barrels tucked into ledges on the cliff face. Making good use of the natural upward draught to keep the fires going, the fish, after being salted and dried, were hung in pairs on poles across the top of the barrels. The whole con-traption was then covered with several layers of hessian sacking which was used to regulate the heat: on dry days with a brisk wind, more layers would be piled on to prevent the fire getting too hot, on wet, windless days the layers would be fewer. Originally, all kinds of surplus fish were smoked in this way but haddock became the most popular. In the early 1800s, a number of Auchmithie fisher-folk settled in Arbroath nearby. They built square, brick smoke-pits in their back gardens, continuing to make the smokie cure. By the end of the century, output from Arbroath greatly exceeded that from Auchmithie and the name of the smokie was changed to reflect this.

Today, the people of Arbroath continue to smoke in their backyards, selling smokies from small shop counters. When the pits are in use, the smell wafting through the streets is overwhelming. Though some prefer to remain small with a single smoke-pit, selling to loyal and regular customers, others have developed a more commercial operation in large plants. They have not, however, managed to reproduce the genuine smokie in computer-operated, high-tech kilns. Those who produce the original continue to work with the old method of small pits covered with sacking. Undoubtedly the best flavour is when the fish is 'hot off the barrel'. Otherwise, it may be split open and the bone removed, the centre filled with butter, and heated in the oven or under a grill. It has been granted Protected Geographical Indication (PGI).

TECHNIQUE:
The fish are gutted, beheaded and dry-salted for about 2 hours, depending on size, to draw excess moisture from the skin and impart a mild salty flavour. They are tied in pairs and hung over wooden rods; the salt is washed off and they are left to dry for about 5 hours to harden the skins. The rods are placed in the smoke-pit and hot-smoked over oak or beech, covered with layers of hessian. Smoking time is approximately 45 minutes.

REGION OF PRODUCTION:
EAST SCOTLAND, ARBROATH (TAYSIDE).

Ayrshire Bacon

DESCRIPTION:

SMOKED OR UNSMOKED CURED PORK FOR COOKING. COLOUR: CREAM FAT, DARK PINK FLESH. FLAVOUR: MILDLY CURED, VERY LIGHTLY SALTED; DEPENDS FOR ITS FLAVOUR ON THE BREED AND QUALITY OF PIG AS WELL AS THE CURE. AYRSHIRE BACON IS MADE FROM GREAT WHITE PREMIUM-GRADE PIGS. BOTH SKIN AND BONES ARE REMOVED BEFORE CURING. THE BACK OR CUTLET PART AND THE STREAKY OR FLANK ARE NOT SEPARATED. ONCE CURED, THE MIDDLE IS ROLLED TIGHTLY, THE FAT SIDE OUTERMOST. THE GIGOT (LEG) IS ROLLED AND TIED AND THE SHOULDER CUT INTO BOILING JOINTS. THESE ARE KNOWN AS AN AYRSHIRE ROLL.

HISTORY:

This is the only distinctive bacon cure in Scotland. It is thought to have arisen in the South West, which has a history of dairying going back at least to the 1600s. In Britain, by-products from the cheese and butter industries have always been used to feed pigs. Potatoes too, grown in south-west Scotland, contributed much to their diet (David Mabey, *In Search of Food*, 1978). Demand may have been stimulated by the presence of many large, wealthy households in the Upper Clyde. Ramsay's of Carluke has been making Ayrshire bacon since 1857 and is now the largest producer.

The bacon was always skinned, boned and rolled. Rolling is necessary because the flank is left attached to the side, giving a very long rasher: the only sensible method for dealing with it is to roll the meat. In contrast to other cures in Britain, the carcasses are not scalded after slaughter. This is because the bristles, normally scraped away with hot water, are removed with the skin. The end product has a finer colour and firmer texture than meat which has been scalded.

The rolled back-bacon is usually cut thinly into rashers and grilled or fried. The round shape of the cut is convenient as a filling for a roll. In the cities of central Scotland, bacon rolls are a popular fast-food – eaten at any time of the day. The gigot is usually cut into steaks for grilling or frying. Both the gigot and the shoulder may be cut into joints for boiling. The term ham in Scotland loosely refers to any kind of bacon and not just the cured leg joint which is the usual English interpretation. In Scotland, this is called cooked ham or gammon.

TECHNIQUE:

Only gilts (young female pigs) of a specified weight are used by Ramsay's. The whole side is boned out and the skin removed. It is wet-brined for 2 days with a small proportion of nitrates for preservation. It is dried for 2–3 weeks before it is cut up and rolled. Some of the production is lightly smoked over oak chips. Some bacon with the back and streaky still in one piece, which has been cured with the skin on and the bone still in, is subsequently skinned, boned and rolled into the Ayrshire cylindrical shape. It is described as Ayrshire-style bacon but is not true Ayrshire. Some Ayrshire bacon curers also cure whole legs on the bone but because the skin and bones have not been removed, neither is this regarded as an authentic Ayrshire cure. The demand for smoked or unsmoked is a local preference. A special spiced cure is made for festive occasions, in small quantities to order.

REGION OF PRODUCTION:
SOUTH WEST SCOTLAND.

Border Tart

DESCRIPTION:
A ROUND OPEN TART 150MM DIAMETER, 20–30MM DEEP; SOMETIMES ICED WITH WHITE GLACÉ ICING, WITH A DARK, DRIED-FRUIT FILLING; ALTERNATIVELY, A RICH SPONGE WITHOUT THE ICING. FLAVOUR: SWEET, RICH WITH DRIED FRUIT, BUTTERY.

The modern Border tart is different from the original casing of yeast dough filled with a rich egg custard and flavoured with marzipan, almonds, lemon and orange peel and sultanas. Border bakers have developed their own, more economical versions. It is now also known as Eyemouth tart and Ecclefechan butter tart.

Sophisticated tarts are thought to have developed in this part of Scotland as a result of the French connection before and immediately after the Act of Union in 1707. Contemporary recipe books show the degree of refinement of Scottish tarts (often described as 'flans') from which the modern Border tart appears to descend. Interpretation by modern bakers has meant styles vary widely. No two are identical. They range from something akin to a Bakewell tart with a rich almond sponge, but which usually includes dried fruit and nuts, to an intensely sweet spongeless filling of fruit, sugar, butter and egg.

TECHNIQUE:

Made with a short-crust pastry case, filled with dried fruit, sugar, melted butter and egg. Alternatively, a sponge-cake filling, including a proportion of ground nuts. When baked and cooled, it is often coated with white glacé icing.

REGION OF PRODUCTION:
SOUTH SCOTLAND, BORDERS.

Cheviot Sheep

DESCRIPTION:
AS WELL AS THE ORIGINAL CHEVIOT, TWO DISTINCT STRAINS ARE RECOGNISED: THE NORTH COUNTRY (IN NORTH ENGLAND AND WEST SCOTLAND) AND THE BRECKNOCK HILL OR SENNYBRIDGE (IN CENTRAL WALES). CARCASSES (DRESSED WEIGHT, IN LATE WINTER) ARE 17–22KG (CHEVIOTS), 25–30KG (NORTH COUNTRY CHEVIOTS). GOOD MEAT CONFORMATION

WITH STRONG SHOULDERS AND BROAD BACKS; CHEVIOTS ARE
SMALLER AND BLOCKIER THAN THE LARGE NORTH COUNTRY
CHEVIOT. LARGE, MEATY SHEEP WHICH YIELD WELL-
FLAVOURED LAMB.

HISTORY:

The breed takes its name from the hills that run along the Scottish border. The primitive 'dun faced' sheep of the Highlands,
noticed in the seventeenth century, was probably an ancestor.
The breed we know today developed in the Northumberland-
Berwick region (S. J. G. Hall & J. Clutton-Brock, *Two Hundred
Years of British Farm Livestock*, 1989). Lincoln rams were used
to improve the strain in the mid-eighteenth century, and some
Leicester blood at the start of the nineteenth. Cheviots had
some reputation by the time Mrs Beeton (1861) commented
on them as providers of wool and meat. The breed society was
founded at the end of the 1800s.

Not long before that, Cheviots were taken south and were
found to do well on the high ground and in the exposed climate
of central Wales. They were also taken north to graze the great
tracts of land available after the Highland Clearances. With
some Merino blood, these developed into a breed known as
North Country Cheviots, or 'Northies'. A breed society for
these was established in 1912.

Cheviot breeds are used for the production of quality lamb.
A first cross is made with Leicester rams, and the female prog-
eny is put to Suffolk, Downland or continental rams to breed
large, lean, fast-maturing lambs. Much of this reaches the market as 'Scottish Lamb'.

TECHNIQUE:

All Cheviot breeds are hardy; the original is still the best for
the bleak hills themselves, which rise to 1,000 metres, with
short grass and little cover for sheep. They live out all year.
Extra feed, usually hay, is only given during the severest condi-

tions and to pregnant ewes in the 6 weeks before lambing in mid-April. Hill lambs are late-maturing; they are killed for meat from August onwards but many are kept as stores on low ground, fed on arable crops and slaughtered in late winter.

The North Country Cheviot has two further strains. One is the Caithness, which, while living further north than the original Cheviot, is not as hardy; it grazes the low ground and rich grass of Caithness. The second is the 'Heather' or Sutherland, an exceptionally hardy, but somewhat smaller, sheep which does well in the harsh climate of western Scotland on unimproved native hill pasture and heather. Cheviot and North Country ewes are much sought by breeders for their excellent mothering qualities. Hill ewes are often sold at about 6 years to lowland farms, where they can be used productively for several more years in a gentler climate.

REGION OF PRODUCTION:
SCOTLAND; NORTH EAST ENGLAND.

Cumnock Tart

DESCRIPTION:
A DOUBLE-CRUST, INDIVIDUAL, SWEET, FRUIT TART 130MM LONG, 100MM WIDE, 30MM DEEP. WEIGHT: ABOUT 110G. COLOUR: SHINY, BROWNED-SUGAR SURFACE WITH LIGHTLY BURNT EDGES. FLAVOUR: FRUITY, SWEET WITH SAVOURY LARD PASTRY.

HISTORY:
This is a regional variation and development of the Scotch pie (a raised pie filled with mutton or beef). The sweet version, using apple or rhubarb, was created by an Ayrshire baker named Stoddart around 1920, using the same savoury lard pastry as the meat pies. The tart was made first in Cumnock (Strathclyde). The second-generation owner of Bradford's bakery in Glasgow, Hugh

Bradford, learned to make it from his father who had been apprenticed to Mr Stoddart. The tart is made to the original recipe for the chain of bakery shops owned by Bradford's.

TECHNIQUE:
Each tart is made from an individual piece of dough which is pinned out by hand to form an oval bottom or base. This is filled with apple or rhubarb. Sugar is added and a thin oval lid placed on top. An edge or rim is formed using the thumb and forefinger while sealing the lid to the base. They are baked for 20–25 minutes. During baking, they are glazed twice with sugar syrup to produce a rich colour and sticky, shiny top.

REGION OF PRODUCTION:
CENTRAL SCOTLAND, GLASGOW.

Dundee Marmalade

DESCRIPTION:
COLOUR: BRIGHT ORANGE THROUGH TO DARK BROWN. COMPOSITION: SEVILLE ORANGES AND SUGAR, SOMETIMES BLACK TREACLE OR BROWN SUGAR. DUNDEE MARMALADE HAS SHREDDED PEEL. WHILE ONCE PRESUMED TO BE MADE WITH ORANGES, MARMALADE IS NOW APPLIED TO ANY CITRUS PRESERVE SUCH AS LIME, GRAPEFRUIT, SWEET ORANGE OR TANGERINE. IT MAY BE FLAVOURED WITH BRANDY, WHISKY, GINGER OR BLACK TREACLE.

HISTORY:
Today, nearly all bitter Seville oranges grown in southern Spain are destined for marmalade for the British market. Pots of marmalade have followed the British around the world for more than a century. In the early 1900s, the Empress of Russia and the Queen of Greece, granddaughters of Queen Victoria, had supplies sent regularly from Wilkins of Tiptree. The firm of Frank Cooper of Oxford still has a tin which was taken on

Scott's expedition to the South Pole in 1911, discovered in perfect condition in 1980. Marmalade has also been taken by the British up Mount Everest.

In the course of its history, marmalade has generated at least a couple of myths for which the Scots must accept some responsibility. One involves the belief that it gets its name from Mary, Queen of Scots. Another is that it was an invention of Janet Keiller, whose Dundee family built the first marmalade factory in 1797. Marmalade made its first appearance in both Scotland and England in wooden boxes: a solid, sugary mass of *marmelos* (quinces), exported from Portugal, and first mentioned as 'marmelada' in port records at the end of the fifteenth century. This is what travelled with Mary Queen of Scots when she became seasick on the crossing from Calais to Scotland in 1561 and which may – or may not – have helped restore her equilibrium. Quinces were regarded at the time as healing fruits. Her request, 'Marmelade pour Marie malade,' was no more than a medicinal pun.

The medicinal properties of oranges were also highly regarded. Candied orange peel was eaten during a fast, so it was a natural thing to pulp and sweeten oranges into a 'marmelade'. It first appears in seventeenth-century English cookery books when it was eaten as a sweetmeat to aid digestion. Now enter the Scots. Until about 1700, a bowl of ale with some toast floating in it had been regarded as the most warming way to start the day. Then came the tea revolution and thereafter tea and crisp toast was the meal *de rigueur*. If it was not to be floated or dunked, this toast required an accompaniment. A solution came in a bargain-load of bitter oranges from Spain, bought by Janet Keiller's husband from a boat in Dundee harbour. This she made into a preserve. According to her English recipe, you pounded and pulped, with much patience, with a pestle and mortar. Instead, she decided to use a French way which was quicker and which chopped the peel into shreds. With a shrewd eye to economy, she decided not to reduce this 'marmelade' to a concentrated paste but to make it less solid, which produced many more pots per pound. It was cooked for a shorter time, improving the flavour and making it easier to spread on toast.

The epicurean traveller, Bishop Richard Pococke (1704–65), indicates the use of what appears to have been marmalade for spreading on toast at breakfast: 'They always bring toasted bread, and besides, butter, honey and jelly of currants and preserved orange peel.'

TECHNIQUE:

In Mrs E. Cleland (*A New and Easy Method of Cookery*, 1755) a recipe appears for shredded orange marmalade: 'To make a Marmalade of Oranges – Take your Oranges, grate them, cut them in quarters, take the skins off them, and take the pulp from the strings and seeds; put the skins in a pan of spring-water, boil them till they are very tender, then take them out of the water, and cut them and leave the thin slices to boil by themselves. To every pound of oranges put a pound of fine sugar, first wet the sugar in water, boil it a good while then put in half of the pulp, keep the other half for the sliced orange; to every mutchkin of the pulp you must put in a pound of sugar likeways, then put in the grated rind, boil till it is very clear, then put in Gallypots; when cold paper them.'

The fruit is softened by boiling on its own. It may be left whole or chopped before boiling. The pulp and water is measured and for every 500ml of pulp, 500g sugar is added. The pips are usually kept separate, but included in the boiling to aid setting, before the fruit is finely chopped. The marmalade is boiled until it sets. Seville oranges are harvested in January, and much marmalade is made at this time.

REGION OF PRODUCTION:
EASTERN SCOTLAND.

Dunlop Cheese

DESCRIPTION:

PASTEURIZED, HARD, COW'S MILK CHEESE, DISTINGUISHED FROM SCOTTISH CHEDDAR AS 'MEATIER', WITH A MORE MELLOW, NUTTY FLAVOUR AND SOFTER, CREAMIER TEXTURE. COLOUR: PALE YELLOW. FORM: ROUNDS FROM 2KG.

HISTORY:

The lowlands of Ayrshire form a crescent along 70 miles of the Firth of Clyde. The warm, wet winds, and the clay and heavy loam soil have combined to grow the most succulent pasture, making this the largest dairying area in the country and the home of Ayrshire cattle, first known as Dunlops or Cunninghams.

Until the late seventeenth century, cheese had been essentially a short-keeping by-product of butter-making, made from the skimmed milk of both cow and sheep. Around 1690, however, a farmer's daughter and Covenanter from Ayrshire, Barbara Gilmour, is said to have returned home after a period of exile in Ulster fleeing religious persecution. She brought with her a recipe for making cheese which revolutionized the product. Instead of using skimmed milk, she used full-cream cow's milk, pressing the cheese until it was quite hard and improving both the keeping quality and the flavour. While the old cheese was described as 'common cheese', the new cheese became known as a 'sweet-milk cheese' or 'new milk cheese'. By the 1790s, when parish accounts were compiled for the Statistical Account of Scotland, it had become a Dunlop cheese, identified as being manufactured in 5 Ayrshire and 2 Lanarkshire parishes.

The rise of Dunlop to more than local significance relates to the growth of the cities of central Scotland, particularly Glasgow and Paisley. The cheese was further improved in 1885 when the Ayrshire Agricultural Association brought a Somerset farmer and his wife to the country to teach the Cheddar method. Original

Dunlop was still being made by at least 300 farms in the South West of Scotland in 1930: 'Each farm had a fully matured cheese open for cooking, and a softer one for eating. At breakfast, porridge was followed on alternate days by bacon and eggs or toasted cheese on a scone made of home-ground flour eaten in front of the fire' (Patrick Rance, *The Great British Cheese Book*, 1982).

The subsequent decline – though not extinction – of Dunlop was a result of developments during and after World War II: milk was bought in bulk from farms by Milk Marketing Boards (MMB) and trucked to large creameries to make factory Cheddar. Its position was further undermined when the MMB took Cheddar rather than Dunlop as the name for their creamery cheeses, believing that Dunlop presented the wrong image, since it happened to have the same name as a leading rubber tyre company of the day, now defunct. Only in some creameries, notably on some of the islands, particularly on Arran, did they retain the Dunlop name and tradition. Elsewhere, Scottish cheese took the Cheddar tag though there have been moves recently to restore Dunlop to its traditional role as a Scottish cheese of distinguished ancestry.

TECHNIQUE:

Made from pasteurized cow's milk. Commercially, it follows the basic Cheddar method but is pressed for a shorter time and matured 4–12 months (average 6 months). An historical recipe is given by F. M. McNeill (*The Scots Kitchen*, 1929): 'As soon as the milk is taken from the cows it is poured into a large pail, or pails, and before it is quite cold the substance called the steep, i.e. rennet, is mixed with it. When it is sufficiently coagulated it is cut transversely with a broad knife made for the purpose, or a broad three-toed instrument, in order to let the curd subside and to procure the separation of the whey from it. When this separation is observed to have taken place, the curd is lifted with a ladle, or something similar, into the chessel where it remains a few hours, till it has acquired something of a hardness or consistency. It is then taken out of the cheese press and cut into small pieces with the instrument above mentioned, of the size of 1 or 2 cubic inches, after which it receives the due proportion of salt, and is again replaced in the chessel and put into the press, where it remains a few hours again. Then it is taken out a second time, cut as before and mixed thoroughly, so that every part may receive the benefit of the salt; and for the last time it is put into the cheese press where it remains till replaced by its successor. After this is done it must be laid in a clean and cool place till sufficiently dried and fit to be carried to market; great care is to be used in frequent turning and rubbing, both to keep the cheese dry and clean and to preserve it from swelling and bursting with the heat, vulgarly "fire-fanging". When these cheeses are properly made and dried as they ought to be, they have a rich and delicious flavour.'

REGION OF PRODUCTION:

SCOTLAND, AYRSHIRE, SOUTH WEST AND SOME ISLANDS.

Edinburgh Rock

DESCRIPTION:

STICKS 10–15MM DIAMETER, 120–140MM LONG. COLOURS AND FLAVOURS: THERE ARE 7 CUSTOMARY TYPES, WHITE (VANILLA), PINK (RASPBERRY, STRAWBERRY), GREEN (LIME), FAWN (GINGER), LEMON (YELLOW) AND ORANGE. COMPOSITION: SUGAR, WATER, COLOUR AND FLAVOURINGS. IT HAS A POWDERY, CRYSTALLIZED TEXTURE.

HISTORY:

Edinburgh rock is said to have been discovered accidentally by a nineteenth-century Edinburgh confectioner, Alexander Ferguson, popularly known as 'Sweetie Sandy'. He found some rock which had been left uncovered in the warm atmosphere of the sweet factory for several months. The rock had crystallized to a brittle texture and its pleasant crunch and delicate flavour became so popular that it was the foundation of Ferguson's business. He became one of Edinburgh's most successful confectioners.

However, the technique of pulling sugar and then allowing it to grain has been known for many centuries, and a mid-fifteenth-century sugar-boiling text of northern provenance, in archives held in the City of York, gives instructions for making 'penides', or sugar sticks. At the end of the recipe, the confectioner is told to leave them in a warm place to take the toughness off them (i.e. to allow them to soften by graining). Whether Ferguson rediscovered this or built on an older tradition is not clear. This rock is now made by many confectioners and is sold throughout the country.

TECHNIQUE:

In many sweets, the confectioner makes strenuous efforts to avoid 'graining' (recrystallization of the sugar once manufacture is complete). In Edinburgh rock, the reverse is true and graining is positively encouraged by omitting ingredients such as acids and adding seed crystals in the form of powdered sugar to the boiled mixture. A batch commences by mixing sugar and water, and boiling it to 130°C (hard ball); it is then poured on to a slab. The flavourings are added and the sugar is dusted with icing sugar and 'pulled' until it hardens, when it is set in the rock shape. The pieces of rock are coated in icing sugar and left in a warm atmosphere until the rock becomes powdery. This takes 1–7 days. Rock with added glucose is made by some but is not regarded as authentic as it produces a 'claggie' (sticky) texture.

REGION OF PRODUCTION:

South Scotland.

Finnan Haddock

DESCRIPTION:

A WHOLE HADDOCK, WITH THE HEAD REMOVED BUT THE BONE LEFT IN, SPLIT, BRINED AND SMOKED. COLOUR: PALE STRAW THROUGH TO GOLDEN BROWN; NO ARTIFICIAL DYE IS USED. FLAVOUR: LIGHTLY SALTED, DELICATELY SMOKED.

HISTORY:

A salt-cured haddock, known as a spelding, can be traced back to the sixteenth century when they are mentioned in the household book of King James V. They are also mentioned by Robert Fergusson in his poem *The Leith Races* (1773), 'Guid speldins, fa will buy'. In the same year, James Boswell describes them in his diary as, 'salted and dried in a particular manner, being dipped in the sea and dried in the sun, and eaten by the Scots by way of a relish'. He also says they were available in London. Speldings, however, were heavily salted and the subsequent move towards a lightly salted, smoked haddock began as communications improved and fish which might otherwise spoil could be delivered with enough dispatch. Due to the reputation of curers who smoked, as well as salted, fish in the village of Findon a few miles south of Aberdeen, the cured fish became known as a Finnan. It is also said that their reputation spread quickly through the country because they were transported to a dealer in Edinburgh by a relation who was guard on the Aberdeen to Edinburgh stage-coach at the beginning of the nineteenth century (John Dyson, *Business in Great Waters*, 1977).

They are mentioned by Robert Southey in his *Journal of a Tour in Scotland* (1819): 'A good breakfast as usual in Scotland, with Findon Haddocks, eggs, sweetmeats, and honey.' Included in the fishwife's creel of smoked and fresh fish, they were hawked about the country during the heyday of the east coast fisheries and became common fare, cooked simply in milk and butter or made into the fishwife's soup-stew, admired throughout the country as a Cullen Skink. The reputation of Finnan haddock suffered in the 1870s when the cure was spoiled by the use of bad peat and a resinous, soft-wood sawdust, making the fillets acrid. It recovered its celebrity and quality, though not without competition from alternative modern cures using artificial dyes, 'painted ladies'. Sometimes described as a 'Golden' fillet, the lightly brined and lightly smoked skinless haddock or whiting should not be confused with the Finnan. A variation with more integrity is the undyed Aberdeen fillet, or smoked fillet, which can be used in the same way as the bone-in Finnan.

TECHNIQUE:

The original Finnans were split with the bone on the left-hand side of the fish, looking at the cut surface with the tail downwards. They were dry-salted overnight and smoked over soft 'grey' peat for 8–9 hours then cooled and washed in warm salted water. Other original Finnan cures around the country included Eyemouth and Glasgow 'Pale' which was a much milder paler cure, smoked for only 30 minutes to 2 hours and split with the bone on the right-hand side. A Moray Firth Finnan was split like a 'Pale' but smoked for about 12 hours making it a much darker, more heavily smoked fish. Methods today vary from commercially produced large-scale smoking in Torry kilns to small independent smokers, using simpler equipment.

REGION OF PRODUCTION:
NORTH EAST AND CENTRAL SCOTLAND.

Forfar Bridie

DESCRIPTION:
A HORSESHOE-SHAPED, BAKED BEEF AND ONION PASTY, WEIGHING 200–750G. COLOUR: PALE BROWN. FLAVOUR: SAVOURY BEEF AND ONIONS.

Third-generation bridie-baker in Forfar, William McLaren, believes that his family's account of the origins of the bridie is more credible than the much-quoted story of Margaret Bridie of Glamis, renowned for her meat pasties which she sold in the Buttermarket in Forfar. According to McLaren, the bridie was a speciality of Jolly's bakery where his grandfather, James McLaren, served his time and learned to make them. This was in the late 1890s and meat was not commonly eaten by the majority of the population: the staple diet was based on porridge and brose, 3 times a day, Sundays and holidays included. Bridies were for special occasions, the horseshoe shape a lucky symbol eaten at the bride's meal, or wedding feast. The lucky bridie continues to be eaten at weddings, also christenings, but has now become a convenient everyday food.

Bridies in Forfar, made to the traditional method, have a high meat content which makes them more expensive than others made elsewhere. In the heart of Aberdeen-Angus country, people reckon lots of meat is essential to eating quality and are critical of any compromises. With a sausage-type filling and without onions, bridie has also become a generic name across Scotland for a crescent-shaped item made with puff pastry. This is not recognized in Forfar as authentic. They are eaten hot, for high tea or lunch with beans and bread and butter.

TECHNIQUE:

Jolly's nineteenth-century recipe (McNeill, 1929): 'Take a pound of the best steak. Beat it with the paste roller, then cut it into narrow strips, and again cut these into one-inch lengths and season with salt and pepper. Divide into three portions. Mince finely three ounces of suet. Make a stiff dough with flour, water and a seasoning of salt, and roll out thin into three ovals. Cover the half of each oval with meat; sprinkle with the suet and a little minced onion if desired. Wet the edges, fold over, and crimp with the finger and thumb. Nip a small hole on top of each. Bake for about half an hour in a quick oven and they will come out golden brown dappled beauties, fit for a king's supper.'

The modern recipe includes mincing the beef through a large plate to give a coarser texture than for pies, mixing with the other ingredients, then following the Jolly method of shaping the pastry and filling. Modern pastry recipes include a fat. Bridies are baked in a hot oven for about 40 minutes depending on size.

REGION OF PRODUCTION:
EAST SCOTLAND, FORFAR (TAYSIDE).

Galloway Cattle

DESCRIPTION:
AVERAGE LIVE WEIGHT FOR 16-MONTH STEER, 470KG. FLESH DEEPLY RED WITH LIGHT MARBLING OF INTRA-MUSCULAR CREAM FAT. FLAVOUR AT ITS BEST WHEN IT HAS BEEN HUNG 2–3 WEEKS.

HISTORY:
Though their subsequent bloodlines followed very different paths, the two modern Scottish breeds of black, hornless beef cattle – the Aberdeen-Angus and the Galloway – have superficial similarities which reflect descent from the same primitive stock. But while the first has responded to intensive feeding, resulting in a rapidly maturing animal, the Galloway has made the most of marginal and hill lands in the South West of Scotland by producing a more slowly maturing breed.

During the eighteenth century, Galloway was a major source of store cattle which were taken by drovers to be fattened in Norfolk or Suffolk for the London market. By the mid-nineteenth, however, the droving trade had ended as beef breeds were developed for supplying Smithfield direct with carcass meat (see Aberdeen-Angus, p. 41). South-Western cattle farmers, therefore, turned to dairying, and the beef cattle were forced to live in the hills.

The Galloway Cattle Society was formed in 1877 in Castle Douglas, still the headquarters of the breed. Until its inception, the polled Angus or Aberdeen cattle and the Galloways were entered in the same herd book, but with the founding of the society the copyright of the Galloway portion was purchased.

During World War II the value of the pure-bred Galloway for hill grazing was recognised and numbers were expanded with Government encouragement. While the breed has maintained its position, despite subsequent changes in Government policy, its most recent history has been significantly affected, once again, by its ability to forage on rough ground without too much expense, making it attractive at a time of rising costs. A variant is the Belted Galloway, so called for the vertical white stripe on its body.

Most Galloways are in southern Scotland with a concentration in the South West; there are some in Cumbria and other parts of the north of England and a few elsewhere in England and Ireland.

TECHNIQUE:
The cattle are out-wintered and maintained on exposed hill and marginal land. They thrive and produce on low-cost rations in winter and in summer on unimproved rough grazing. They are particularly suited to extensive husbandry.

REGION OF PRODUCTION:
SOUTH WEST SCOTLAND.

Glasgow Roll

DESCRIPTION:

A SQUARISH MORNING ROLL WITH HARD OUTER SURFACE, 100MM LONG, 50MM HIGH. WEIGHT: 40G. COLOUR AND TEXTURE: FROM LIGHT BROWN THROUGH TO ALMOST BLACK ON THE SURFACE OF A BURNT ROLL; A LIGHT, OPEN, WELL-AERATED TEXTURE WHICH IS NONE THE LESS CHEWY. FLAVOUR: SALTY.

HISTORY:

This is a local form of the morning roll which developed its hard outer crust and airy, non-doughy, centre for the special purpose of holding bacon or a fried egg (or both at once) as a worker's breakfast. They were eaten in large quantities by men in places such as the Clydeside shipyards, as well as other local industries, as the mid-morning snack. The roll was popular because of its robust quality. Alternative names were hard rolls and burnt rolls – so requested by those who liked their bread very well fired. Glasgow rolls are torn open rather than cut.

TECHNIQUE:

The dough is made with 100 per cent Canadian high-protein flour, mixed with water, liquid malt, yeast, and salt, and bulk fermented for 4–5 hours. Shaping is still done by hand, even in some large bakeries; final proving is also relatively extended. The rolls are baked for 14 minutes at 240°C.

REGION OF PRODUCTION:
CENTRAL SCOTLAND, GLASGOW.

Irn-Bru

DESCRIPTION:

IRN-BRU IS ORANGE-GOLDEN IN COLOUR, ITS FLAVOUR SWEET-SPICY WITH A CITRUS TANG, RATHER LIKE BOILED SWEETS. IT CONTAINS AMMONIUM FERRIC CITRATE (0.002 PER CENT). THIS FORTIFICATION WITH IRON DISTINGUISHES IT FROM OTHER SOFT DRINKS.

HISTORY:

Prior to the development of twentieth-century medicines, herbalists made cordials and tonics, giving rise to a number of 'health' drinks. This tradition, combined with a strong temperance movement in the early decades of the twentieth century was a source of many patent bottled drinks made under brand names by various companies. 'Iron-Brew' was a common mixed-flavour drink developed in Scotland during the early 1900s and was made by several manufacturers, each with a different recipe. Few actually contained iron.

All these drinks were affected by changes brought about by World War II. Iron brews disappeared as the industry was rationalized and companies became numbered production units. After the war, legislation was passed which made it compulsory to add 0.125g of iron per fluid ounce (30ml) to any beverage named iron-brew. There was also a rumour that the Government was planning to ban the misuse of terms like brew which did not actually apply to a brewing process. Because of this, and the fact that Barr's recipe did not contain the necessary amount of iron, in 1946 the then chairman of A.G. Barr decided to overcome the problem by registering the phonetic 'Irn-Bru' as a trade name. At the same time, a major advertising campaign with a cartoon strip depicting the adventures of 'Ba-Bru and Sandy' was inserted in one of Glasgow's main newspapers, the *Bulletin*, and ran until the 1970s. Other companies producing iron brews did not survive but Barr's Irn-Bru became so successful that it has now taken the title 'Scotland's other drink'. It is carried around the world by nostalgic Scots – particularly to football matches where Scotland's other drink is not allowed.

TECHNIQUE:

The flavourings that give these drinks their distinctive character are closely-guarded trade secrets. The ingredients for Irn-Bru are water, sugar, carbon dioxide, citric acid, flavourings, preservative (E211), caffeine, colours (E110, E124), ammonium ferric citrate (0.002 per cent). Manufacture follows the standard method for all carbonated drinks: the flavouring and colouring ingredients are mixed to make a syrup which is combined with water and sugar, carbonated and bottled.

REGION OF PRODUCTION:

CENTRAL SCOTLAND, GLASGOW.

Kale

DESCRIPTION:

KALE HAS NO HEART BUT GROWS ON A LONG STEM WITH
CURLED FINELY DENTED LEAVES. COLOUR: DARK GREEN.
FLAVOUR: CHANGES FROM MILD TO MORE INTENSELY SPICY
AFTER IT HAS BEEN FROSTED.

HISTORY:

Kale was originally a staple, surviving well in a harsh winter,
consumed throughout northern Europe. The word cole,
i.e. kale, used generically for members of the brassica family,
stems first from the Latin, *caulis*. Similar derivations are widespread in European languages, from the Welsh *cawl*, to the
German *Kohl*. Borecole is curly kale, an improved variety taken
from the Dutch, where it was called *boerenkool*, 'peasant's
cabbage'. In the same way, hearted cabbage was sometimes
called cabbage-cole (from the French *caboche*, head).

The kail-yard (kitchen garden) was to the Scots (particularly
in the Lowlands) what the potato-plot was to the Irish peasant.
Kail was so inextricably linked with eating, that the midday
meal became known as 'kail'. The bells of St Giles Cathedral in
Edinburgh which chimed at dinner-time (in the eighteenth
century at 2 o'clock) were known as the 'Kail-bells'. In Meg
Dods (*The Cook and House-wife's Manual*, 1826), Scotland is
referred to as 'The Land o' Kail'. So attached is the word to a
particular vision of the country that 'kail-yaird' has been applied
to a school of fiction which depicts Scottish village life. Two
practitioners were Sir James Barrie and S.R. Crockett.

While the Scots used the spelling kail, the northern English
called it cale. Today, it is known in Scotland and the rest of
Britain as kale and the Scots continue to use it in broths, or as
a vegetable, while in England it has largely remained winter
feed for cattle.

The advantage of kale for Scottish growers is that it is hardy. Also, it has the rare quality in a vegetable of benefiting from periods of frost. In a normal Scottish winter, several frosts, the duration and number depending on altitude, aspect and the general weather, can be expected, so any vegetable resistant to these is useful.

Traditional varieties such as Green Curled and Thousand Headed Kale are little grown, although efforts to preserve their genetic material is carried on by a dedicated band. F1 hybrids, which crop uniformly and reliably, are now favoured. Commercially, kale is grown from seed in mid-May to early July for winter use. It is less hardy in rich soils. Older methods of growing survived in the Orkneys into the 1970s, the seed being sown in plantie crubs – specially constructed enclosures of turf or stone in the common grazings. In April, the growing plants were transferred to kaleyards near the houses to grow on to maturity (A. Fenton, 'Traditional Elements in the diet of the Northern Isles of Scotland', 1973).

REGION OF PRODUCTION:
GENERAL SCOTLAND, SOUTH EAST SCOTLAND, FIFE AND LOTHIAN.

Moffat Toffee

DESCRIPTION:
A DARK BROWN SWEET WITH AN ASTRINGENT, SHERBET-LIKE CENTRE, MEASURING 125MM ACROSS.

HISTORY:
The enthusiasm for sugar confectionery in Scotland developed to a peak in the Victorian period as ships loaded with sugar from the West Indies sailed up the Clyde to be refined in Greenock, popularly known as 'Sugaropolis'.

Making a living from sweetie-boiling became a common occupation for many small traders. They would boil up a few pans of sugar in the back shop. Janet Keiller – of marmalade fame – is reputed to have used her sweetie-boiling pans to make her first marmalade. Though many of the colourful and unusual sweets hawked round the streets and markets have not survived the passing of their original makers, remnants of this tradition exist in a number of distinctive local confections.

The recipe for Moffat Toffee has been in Blair Blacklock's family for at least 3 generations. Its origins, however, have been lost and no more can be said than that Mr Blacklock remembers his great-grandmother making sweets. The toffee is largely sold in the family sweet shop in the centre of Moffat.

TECHNIQUE:
The sugar is boiled to 148°C (hard crack). Some of the mixture is poured onto a slab and worked or pulled on a pulling machine to aerate it and lighten the colour. It would appear that it is at this point that the 'secret' ingredient is added. This flavoured and lighter mixture is then encased in the original, and pulled into thin sticks which are cut into sweets.

REGION OF PRODUCTION:
SOUTH WEST SCOTLAND, MOFFAT (DUMFRIES AND GALLOWAY).

Paving Stone

DESCRIPTION:
A LONG, NARROW BISCUIT, LIKE A CYLINDER CUT IN HALF LENGTHWAYS, ABOUT 70MM LONG, AND 20MM HIGH AT THE THICKEST POINT, TAPERING TOWARDS THE ENDS. COLOUR: MID-BROWN, CONTAINING CURRANTS, WITH SUGARY WHITE OUTER COATING. FLAVOUR AND TEXTURE: SPICY, QUITE SWEET, WITH AN AERATED, HARD TEXTURE WHICH SOFTENS A LITTLE ON KEEPING.

The origin of these biscuits, a type of gingerbread, is unknown. Made in eastern Central Scotland, they appear to be the speciality of one company, which was founded in 1919, which has been making them ever since. Many recipes for crisp gingerbreads are to be found in Scotland. Edinburgh, not far to the south of Fife, was famous for its Parliament cakes. Parkins, hard gingerbread biscuits which soften on keeping, are also known in the south and east of Scotland. The coating of grained sugar given to Paving Stones seems to be unique in British cookery.

TECHNIQUE:

The exact method is a trade secret, but the biscuits call for a dough based on creamed fat and sugar, mixed with flour, spices, baking powder, currants and milk. After baking, boiled sugar is poured on to an oiled slab; the biscuits are placed on top and tossed, using wooden bats, until the sugar grains and forms a white coating on the biscuit surface. The biscuits are separated, cooled and dried.

REGION OF PRODUCTION:
EAST SCOTLAND, FIFE.

Puggie Bun

DESCRIPTION:

AN OVAL BUN COMPOSED OF A FILLING OF GINGER DOUGH EN-
CLOSED IN A PALE CREAMY-GOLD PASTRY CASE WHICH IS
SLASHED 4 TIMES ACROSS THE TOP; ABOUT 90MM LONG,
70MM WIDE, 15–25MM DEEP. FLAVOUR AND TEXTURE: DOUGHY,
PASTRY DRY-TEXTURED; CRUMBLY, GINGER-FLAVOURED
FILLING.

HISTORY:

The name is of unknown origin. The word 'puggie' or 'puggy',
has several meanings in English and Scots dialects, including
one relating to mixing operations and another (obsolete) a term
of endearment. Whether either of these has anything to do with
this bun is unclear. The alternative name of Gowrie bun, remembered by some older inhabitants in the south-eastern Scottish Highlands, suggests a strong connection with the lowlands
along the north side of the River Tay, a fertile corn-growing
area known as the Carse of Gowrie, near where these buns are
still produced.

The puggie bun is an outer wrapping of plain pastry which
hides a spiced and sweet filling which is almost equal quantities
of treacle or syrup and flour. There are strong precedents for
pastry-wrapped goods of this type in the baking traditions of
the British Isles; the one which is most relevant in this context
is probably the Scottish black bun, a large cake of dried fruit
wrapped in pastry. The filling for puggie buns is a substance
called gundy dough by the bakers who make it (gundy is an old
Scottish word for a spiced sweetmeat). It is a very similar mixture to one used for an old Scottish speciality, no longer made,
which was a type of gingerbread called parleys, or parliament
cakes. J. Kirkland (*The Modern Baker, Confectioner and Caterer*,
1907) comments that the dough for these 'was invariably made
up in large quantities, and stocked in barrels, to be worked up

afterwards as required'. Although these buns were apparently well known in central Scotland in the past, only one baker (in Cupar, Fife) has been located who produces them. He remarks that they are most popular with older people, who eat them as a snack or for tea, cut in half and spread with butter.

TECHNIQUE:
A gundy dough is made up from flour, syrup and spices and stored for use as needed. Pastry is made up fresh using a hot-water method and beef dripping as the fat. When required, the gundy dough is scaled off and shaped into balls; the pastry is wrapped around and sealed. The bun is turned so the join in the pastry is underneath and pinned or rolled further until the correct oval shape is achieved. The top is slashed. During baking the bun rises and the slashes open to reveal the filling; they are deliberately baked until rather dry. The gundy dough used to be raised with a mixture of pearlash and alum. At the turn of the century, bakers converted to bicarbonate of soda.

REGION OF PRODUCTION:
EAST CENTRAL SCOTLAND.

Selkirk Bannock

DESCRIPTION:
A WEIGHTY, ROUNDED BUN, FLAT ON THE BOTTOM AND CURVED ON TOP, 150–200MM DIAMETER, MADE IN SMALL AND LARGE SIZES. WEIGHT: 450G (SMALL)–800G (LARGE). COLOUR: GOLD. FLAVOUR: RICH BUTTERY YEAST BREAD FLAVOURED WITH SULTANAS.

HISTORY:
The word bannock referred originally to a round, unleavened dough the size of a meat plate which was baked on the girdle and used by the oven-less Scots in place of yeast-raised, oven-baked bread. The word in Old Scots, *bannok,* is thought to

'...*bannocks and a share of cheese*
Will make a breakfast that a laird might please.'

ALLAN RAMSAY, 'THE GENTLE SHEPHERD'

come from Latin, probably through the influence of the Church and may have originally referred to Communion bread. It is now generally used to described any baked item which is large and round.

A Selkirk baker, Robbie Douglas, opened a shop on the Market Place in 1859 and so impressed his customers with the quality of his rich yeasted bannocks that in time they took the name of Selkirk. He discovered that the finished flavour was greatly influenced by the quality of the butter and, after some experimenting, found the best came from cows grazing on neighbouring pastures. He used only the best sultanas from Turkey and together with his baking skills produced the legendary bannock. On her visit to Sir Walter Scott's granddaughter at Abbotsford in 1867, Queen Victoria refused all else of the sumptuous baking save a slice of the Douglas bannock.

While a number of bakers now make the bannock, the original Douglas recipe is said to have come down from Alex Dalgetty, one of the bakers who worked with Douglas. Dalgetty's descendants continue to make the 'original' at their bakery in Galashiels, though Houston's in Hawick now owns the actual bakery where Douglas worked. Hossack's in Kelso has recently developed the Tweed Bannock using wholemeal flour.

Once an everyday bread dough, bakers now make up a special bannock dough. Some, but not all, continue to follow the original method of a 'sponge' which leaves the dough overnight for slower fermentation and development of a finer, more mature flavour.

TECHNIQUE:
Yeast dough is made up with about 4 parts flour to 1 part butter and lard. It is left to rise and then knocked back with 1 part sugar and 2 parts sultanas added.

REGION OF PRODUCTION:
SOUTH SCOTLAND, BORDERS.

Softie

DESCRIPTION:

A ROUNDED BUN 100MM DIAMETER, 40MM HIGH. WEIGHT: 50–60G. COLOUR: GOLDEN. FLAVOUR: SLIGHTLY SWEET.

HISTORY:

This bun appears to have taken its name mainly to distinguish it from the Aberdeen butterie or rowie (see p. 43) and is also sold as a morning roll. The fact that the rowie is a harder, crisper product gave rise to the term softie. This, at least, is one interpretation. An alternative name was soft biscuit: a literal description of their quality and the word biscuit describing a small roll or cake – a similar usage may be found in Guernsey (Elizabeth David, *English Bread and Yeast Cookery*, 1977) and in North America. Though there is no written evidence, an Aberdeenshire baker of over 50 years' experience has established that softies and rowies have been common since the early 1900s. Production has spread beyond Aberdeen, down the east coast and Fife to Edinburgh. Because they contain more sugar than baps or rowies, and less fat than rowies, they are most commonly eaten at tea or supper with preserves, but may also be used as an envelope for savoury fillings. A. L. Simon, (*The Concise Encyclopaedia of Gastronomy*, 1960) records their being toasted for rusks.

TECHNIQUE:

Softies contain double the sugar used in a bap. Otherwise, the doughs are similar.

REGION OF PRODUCTION:

EAST SCOTLAND.

Starry Rock

DESCRIPTION:

STICKS, 120MM LONG, 70–100MM DIAMETER. WEIGHT: 15G.
COLOUR: PALE YELLOW-GOLD. FLAVOUR: SWEET, SLIGHTLY
LEMON.

HISTORY:

Starry Rock is an old-fashioned sweet of the same type as
barley sugar. Recipes appear in many early manuals and it was
probably widespread during the 1800s. In the small Scottish
town of Kirriemuir, this sweet has been known as Starry Rock
since 1833, when the shop which still sells it was established.
The present owner says the recipe is always sold with the shop.
Older people in the town remember with great affection 'Starry
Annie', who could be seen making the rock in the front of the
shop early last century.

TECHNIQUE:

A mixture of sugar, Golden Syrup, water and a little fat is boiled
to a very high temperature; secret flavouring essence is added.
The mixture is poured on a marble slab and worked a little, then
pulled out by hand to make sticks and cut into appropriate
lengths.

REGION OF PRODUCTION:

EASTERN SCOTLAND, KIRRIEMUIR (TAYSIDE).

Italian (Tally's) Ice-Cream

DESCRIPTION:

CLASSIC SCOTTISH 'ITALIAN' VANILLA ICE-CREAM IS USUALLY
MADE ENTIRELY OF MILK AND IS THEREFORE LESS CREAMY
THAN THOSE ICES WITH A RICHER CREAM CONTENT. IT IS
ALSO SLIGHTLY COLDER AND MORE ICY, TAKING LONGER TO
FREEZE. THIS GIVES IT AN INCREASED DENSITY, WHICH HAS
THE EFFECT OF INTENSIFYING THE FLAVOUR TO SOMETHING
WHICH IS CLEAR, CLEAN, LIGHT AND WHOLLY MILKY.

HISTORY:

This is the product of the 'Tallys', Italian cafés which are a feature of Scottish high streets. The first Italians came to Britain in the 1850s but, by the end of the century, as economic conditions worsened in Italy, the trickle of immigrants became a flood. Recruited by agents of masters in London, they were hired as cheap labour. In winter they worked as hurdy-gurdy men, but in summer they cranked and froze the ice-cream mix they had made the previous night.

According to Bruno Sereni in *They Took the Low Road* (1973), the first Italians to arrive in Glasgow were from the Ciociana district, and they were responsible for laying the foundations of what was to become a flourishing ice-cream (and fish-and-chip) industry in Scotland. 'With great courage and initiative, in the space of about seventy years (1850–1920), they had graduated from itinerant begging … to itinerant ice-cream salesmen … to owners of shops in slum quarters … to proprietors of luxurious ice-cream parlours in Sauchiehall Street with mirrors on the walls and wooden partitions between the leather-covered seats.'

As the Italian ice-cream trade developed, a hierarchy was established with the most prosperous playing a major role in the training and careers of many of the young immigrants. They started at the bottom of the ladder and worked up to the ownership of a shop. Itinerant ice-cream selling continued (as it still does) but many more Italian cafés were opened, often as part of a chain. Then the individual shops were sold off to employees when they showed that they could make a profit.

This large community of quality Italian ice-cream makers spread themselves about Scotland to such an extent that every town had at least one, if not two, Italian cafés (nicknamed Tallys). Robert McKee ('Ice Cream Vendors', 1991) gave figures which reflect their growing importance: in 1903 there were 89 in Glasgow, a year later 184, and by 1905, 336. Italian ice-cream had become one of the great pleasures of the working classes, and was soon to become socially acceptable to the prissy middle classes as well. Young men like Denis in A.J. Cronin's novel about Glasgow, *Hatter's Castle*, started taking their girlfriends to the forbidden territory of the Tally. Cronin's Mary had expected to find a 'sordid den', but instead there were clean marble-topped tables, shining mirrors, plush stalls and, best of all, seductive ice-cream.

A range of ices became popular, with some borrowing from the American sundae tradition, but most distinctive and persistent was the habit of pouring a raspberry sauce over the ice-cream. One legend has it that it was invented in Glasgow when a supporter of Clyde football club, whose colours are red and white, persuaded his Tally to make a red and white ice-cream. The ice-cream was named 'Macallum' after the supporter. Special 'Macallum Saucers' are remembered, though the raspberry sauce (commonly known as Tally's Blood) is now mostly poured over cones.

The extent to which Scottish tastes have been influenced by this quality ice-cream can be seen in its continued popularity. Before the discovery of soft-scoop ice-cream – made with the maximum amount of air which can be beaten in to increase the volume because it is sold by volume not weight – a post-war generation of Scottish children had tasted the real thing. They had queued at their local Tallys, if not with the family milk-jug for a fill-up of ice-cream in the days when no one had a refrigerator, then certainly for a penny-cone dripping with bright red Tally's blood. The soft-scoop 'whippy' ices were no match for the Tally's ice-cream.

TECHNIQUE:

The ingredients are first pasteurized, i.e. heated at varying temperatures from 60°C upwards. They are then homogenized under pressure, the degree of pressure depending on the percentage of solids in the mix. The mixture is cooled quickly through chilled coils, it is then put into an 'ageing' vat where, again depending on the percentage of solids, the mixture is left to mature. It is then put into the freezer, which may be a batch-type taking about 25 litres at a time, or a continuous freezer. In the batch-type, 40 per cent (and upwards) of air is beaten into the ice-cream; in the continuous freezer it is pumped in. If the amount of air added exceeds 100 per cent, the subsequent amount is known as 'overrun'. Italian ice-cream manufacturers are reluctant to declare the exact percentage of air added, but maintain it is much less than 100 per cent but not quite as low as 40 per cent.

REGION OF PRODUCTION:
CENTRAL SCOTLAND.

North Scotland: North, West, & Highlands & Islands

Aberdeen-Angus Cattle

DESCRIPTION:

AVERAGE CARCASS WEIGHT OF STEER AT 18–19 MONTHS, 275KG. FLESH DEEPLY RED, FAT CREAM-WHITE, MARBLED WITH INTRA-MUSCULAR FAT.

HISTORY:

Though the most widely known Scottish breed, Aberdeen-Angus is also the most recently established. Pioneer breeder Hugh Watson (1780–1865), from Keillor near Dundee, first showed his black, polled cattle in 1820 and by 1829 was sending some of his stock from the Highland Show in Perth to Smithfield. Hitherto, cattle had been exported on the hoof for fattening in East Anglia. Now, the trade to London of prime beef in carcass (sending only the most expensive cuts) developed with the success of Watson's herd. This new method became the norm with the completion of the railway to London in 1850. Watson is regarded as having fixed the type of the new breed and by the time his herd was dispersed, in 1861, it had been highly selected within itself. For the 50 years of its existence, it seems he never bought a bull. He sold stock to William McCombie (1805–1880), of Tillyfour near Aberdeen, who carried on the programme, attaching the same importance to meeting the requirements of the London trade. The breed's main rival was Amos Cruickshank's Scotch Shorthorn, established in the 1830s when he and his brother became tenants of an Aberdeenshire farm. It could be fattened more rapidly, but did not milk so well and was less hardy than the Watson stock. To overcome its problems and to induce more rapid fattening in the Aberdeen-Angus, the characteristics of the breeds were combined. The Aberdeen-Angus cross Shorthorn became the source of most prime beef in Scotland.

The Polled Cattle Herd Book was started in 1862; the Aberdeen-Angus Cattle Society inaugurated in 1879. In 1891, a separate class at the Smithfield Show was provided for the breed and it has never lost its pre-eminence. At the Perth sales in 1963 a single bull made history with a world-record price of 60,000 guineas.

Changes have occurred in the last 30 years. A demand developed in the 1960s for a small, thick bull with a lot of meat. The trend reversed with entry to the EU, since which time the preference has been for taller, leaner animals with a minimum of fat. 'But this meat,' said the breed society president, 'does not have the succulence and flavour that the consumer requires. Thus the aim now is to have meat that has a marbling of fat through it, to give a healthy product that is succulent and tasty.' This has stimulated a new departure, as retailers themselves support the identification of beef as Aberdeen-Angus as a guarantee of quality. A Certification Trade Mark has been registered.

TECHNIQUE:
The breed thrives on low-quality pasture and rations such as silage and arable by-products. It converts these more effectively than most others into high-quality, early-maturing beef with marbled fat, making it both economically and environmentally desirable.

REGION OF PRODUCTION:
NORTH EAST SCOTLAND.

Aberdeen Rowie

DESCRIPTION:

A MISSHAPEN, UNEVEN, VAGUELY ROUND, FLAKY, FLAT BUN ABOUT 10–20MM DEEP, 80MM DIAMETER AND WEIGHING ABOUT 75G. IT IS SOMETIMES LIKENED TO A CROISSANT WITHOUT THE SHAPE. THERE ARE SEVERAL VARIATIONS ON THE ORIGINAL FORM, FOR EXAMPLE WEE ROWIES (TWO-THIRDS THE NORMAL SIZE), DOUBLE ROWIES (STUCK BACK-TO-BACK WITH BUTTER) AND LOAFIES (MADE WITH ROWIE DOUGH, BUT BAKED IN A BATCH PRODUCING A SQUARE, DEEPER ROWIE). IN SOME PARTS THE DOUGH IS THICKER AND MORE BREAD-LIKE THAN THE ABERDEENSHIRE FLAKY, LAYERED, YEASTED PASTRY. COLOUR: DEEP GOLDEN BROWN FOR WELL-FIRED, 'CREMATED' ROWIES TO PALER GOLDEN FOR LESS WELL-FIRED 'PALES'. FLAVOUR: A BURNT SALTINESS WHICH IS LARGELY DE-TERMINED BY THE DEGREE OF FIRING AND THE FLAVOUR OF THE FAT.

HISTORY:

These are thought to have developed as a result of the boom in the fishing industry in Aberdeen around the turn of the last century when an enterprising baker (origin unknown) was asked to make the fishermen a roll which would not go stale during their 2–3 week trips to the fishing grounds. The first literary mention of them is of a street-seller in Arbroath in 1899: 'Between butteries, Rob Roys [a kind of Bath bun], and turnovers, her basket was weel filled.'

Although Aberdeen still has more bakers producing their own distinctive and, they would claim, 'authentic' rowies, others, from Caithness to Edinburgh, sell what they describe as Aberdeen butteries. A rowie, or roll, is how they are commonly referred to in Aberdeen. The term butterie is odd since they are not made with butter. The name seems to have been given to them by non-Aberdonians, aware that they are fatty but not realising that the fat used is not butter. Most bakers use vegetable shortening or lard, though the original fishermen's rowies were made with butcher's dripping.

TECHNIQUE:

Two doughs are made. One very soft and sticky with very little fat and the other stiffer with most of the fat. In large bakeries the 2 batches are mixed by machine for a few seconds only, to preserve the layers. In smaller bakeries they are folded and rolled by hand in the same way as puff pastry, using the sticky dough as if it were the butter. Shaping is invariably by hand. Mechanical devices have been tried: none has been satisfactory. The dough it is divided into approximately 50g pieces which are pressed out first with 4 outstretched, floured fingers, then knocked into their uneven shape with the floured backs of 4 fingers of the left hand and the floured clenched knuckles of the right. Proved in a warm, steamy atmosphere for 20 minutes they are baked for 18–20 minutes in a fairly hot oven. They are left on the tray until stacked on their sides.

REGION OF PRODUCTION:
EAST SCOTLAND.

Beremeal Bannock

DESCRIPTION:
DISCS 150MM DIAMETER, 12MM THICK. COLOUR: LIGHT GREY-BROWN CRUMB, ROUGH, MEALIE CRUST. FLAVOUR: STRONGER THAN PEARL BARLEY FLOUR, THEY HAVE AN ASTRINGENT, EARTHY TANG, UNSWEETENED.

HISTORY:
Barley was the staple cereal crop in Scotland from Neolithic times until it was progressively displaced by oats (introduced by the Romans) and then by wheat, from the seventeenth century. Barley remained the vital ingredient for beer, whisky dis-

tilling, barley broth and barley bannocks; in the Highlands and Islands and among the lower classes in the Lowlands, it continued to be used for making bread. The practice has persisted to this day in the Highland region, particularly in Orkney.

The distinctive form of barley used for bannocks is the variety known as bigg or big (the four-rowed barley, *Hordeum vulgare*). Bigg is called bere or bear (pronounced bare). While the modern bannock is leavened with buttermilk and baking soda, the original was made by cooking the meal first in milk and butter to make a paste. This was then rolled out into thin chapati-like pancakes which were cooked on the girdle or flat iron baking plate. When cooked, they were spread with butter, rolled up tightly and eaten hot. They are still eaten as a savoury part of evening supper in Orkney, accompanied by butter and a slice of fresh, young cheese.

TECHNIQUE:

Modern recipes vary the proportion of beremeal to wheat flour. Most printed Orkney recipes suggest about half and half but some Orcadians make their bannocks with very little wheat flour, preferring the stronger flavour of the beremeal. The flour is mixed with baking soda and buttermilk to make a moist dough which is rolled out and baked on a floured girdle or hot-plate, turning once.

REGION OF PRODUCTION:
NORTH SCOTLAND, ORKNEY.

Caboc Cheese

DESCRIPTION:
SOFT, DOUBLE-CREAM CHEESE ROLLED IN TOASTED PINHEAD OATMEAL TO MAKE LOGS ABOUT 10CM LONG, 4CM DIAMETER. WEIGHT: 125G. COLOUR: CREAM INSIDE, GREY OATMEAL OUTSIDE. FLAVOUR: RICH CREAM, BUTTERY WITH A MILD TANG.

In the period prior to the Highland Clearances the native soft cheese of Viking and Pictish ancestry was made by every crofter with surplus milk. Its demise came with the increase in sheep farming and shooting estates, putting an end to the crofter's system of taking his cattle, sheep and goats to the mountain grazings in summer where the women and children made the peasant cheese known as crowdie (see p. 69).

A recipe for a richer cheese, made for the clan chiefs, is reputed to be the oldest historical record of a traditional Scottish cheese and was passed down through the female line of the descendants of Mariota de Ile, a daughter of a fifteenth-century Macdonald of the Isles. The present descendant, and owner of the recipe, Susanna Stone, has revived the cheese, making it in her creamery in Tain where she began by making the crofters' cheese, crowdie, in the early 1960s.

A pioneer of the post-war farmhouse cheese-making revival, she called the oatmeal-coated chieftain's cheese Caboc, a derivation from the Scots word for any round cheese 'kebbuck'. Others cheese-makers have copied the recipe with varying degrees of success and the cheese is now established in the Scottish speciality cheese market.

TECHNIQUE:

The recipe uses pasteurized milk from cattle on 3 designated farms. This soft, double-cream cheese is made with lactic acid but no rennet and the logs are finished by rolling in toasted pinhead oatmeal before packing. The exact method is a trade secret.

REGION OF PRODUCTION:

SCOTLAND, HIGHLANDS.

Dulse

DESCRIPTION:

A BROAD-LEAVED SEAWEED WHICH GROWS TO ABOUT 30CM. THE YOUNG FRONDS ARE THIN AND PAPERY.; WEIGHT: SOLD IN 50G PACKS. COLOUR: A DEEP REDDISH PURPLE. FLAVOUR: STRONG, SALTY, IODINE AROMA AND FLAVOUR.

HISTORY:

In the Scottish Highlands and Islands, sea vegetables were originally a regular part of the diet; there are 22 Gaelic names for varieties of seaweed: that for dulse is *duileasg*. Gathered from the foreshore, dulse (*Rhodymenia palmata*) was used in broths, deepening the flavour with the seaweed's high content of strongly flavoured amino acids. Dulse was fed raw to children as an important source of vitamins in a harsh climate with limited resources. It was also sold in the nineteenth century along with tangle (*Laminaria digitata* or *saccherina*), in city markets by itinerant street-sellers to the cry of 'Dulse and Tangel'. Oral tradition states that seaweeds of various types were dried to preserve them. In recent years, there has been a revival of sea vegetables for their nutritional qualities and the unpolluted shores around the north of Scotland have begun to be exploited for their abundant seaweeds.

There are 2 variations on dulse: Autumn Dulse is harvested at that season, when the plant is more vibrant, the colour is deeper and the flavour more astringent; there is also Pepper Dulse (*Laurencia pinnatifida*) which is a variety of colours from red-brown to yellow-green and whose fronds measure up to 18cm. Long stems are chewed for their pungent flavour. Other harvested Scottish sea vegetables include dabberlocks, grockle, sugar ware, finger ware, and *sloke* (wild nori), which is laver in Wales.

Picking is direct from the sea bed by divers, who take particular care not to damage new growth. It is harvested just before it becomes fertile and builds up the bitter content which gives an unpleasant taste. It is air-dried in a recirculating drying oven at a low heat to preserve the flavour.

REGION OF PRODUCTION:
NORTH SCOTLAND.

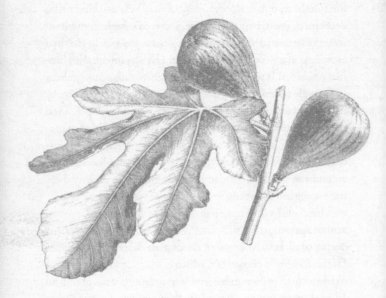

'Dost thou think, because thou art virtuous, there shall be no more cakes and ale?'

WILLIAM SHAKESPEARE, *TWELFTH NIGHT*

Heather Ale

DESCRIPTION:

HEATHER ALE IS AMBER-GOLD AND HAS A FLOWERY, ARO-
MATIC FLAVOUR, WITH A BITTER NOTE. IT IS 4 PER CENT AL-
COHOL BY VOLUME (CASK ALE), 5 PER CENT ALCOHOL BY
VOLUME (BOTTLED VERSION). PICTISH ALE IS 5.4 PER CENT
ALCOHOL BY VOLUME.

HISTORY:

Neolithic remains from the Inner Hebrides include pottery
with residues indicating it had held a fermented beverage containing heather. There are many references from the Middle
Ages onwards to beers brewed with heather and other herbs,
especially bog myrtle. Such drinks survived the introduction of
brewing methods from continental Europe in some areas of the
west and north of Scotland, especially Galloway and the
remoter parts of the Highlands and Islands. The traveller Pen-
nant encountered heather ale in Islay in the eighteenth century,
and F. M. McNeill, writing in 1956, recalls a woman on Orkney
who made it (*The Scots Cellar*). The Islands were remote from
mainstream brewing practices, with no major commercial brewers
until the twentieth century; consequently, the habit of brewing
with local herbs, rather than hops, survived and remains as
a tradition of home-brewing. Recently, heather ale has been
revived as a commercial product by a Glasgow company,
Heather Ale Ltd, who began to develop a recipe translated from
Gaelic in the mid-1980s. It is marketed as 'Fraoch' (pronounced
fruich); *leann fraoch* is Gaelic for heather ale.

TECHNIQUE:

Heather for this beer is gathered from bell heather (*Erica cinerea*)
and ling (*Calluna vulgaris*), 2 species native to the British Isles. It
is cut during the flowering season, in shoots 8–10cm long, including the young leaves and flowers. To make the beer, Scotch
ale malt is sparged (sprayed with hot water) to extract the malt

sugars, giving a solution called wort. The wort is boiled in a brew kettle, to which heather and a small quantity of hops are added; after boiling, the mixture is run through a hop-back (sieve) in which fresh heather is placed. Brewer's yeast is added, and the wort allowed to ferment for several days, depending on the alcoholic strength desired; more heather flowers are laid on the top during this time. The beer is conditioned in bulk for about 10 days until the appropriate carbon dioxide level is reached; during this process it is fined and then filtered into casks or bottles as appropriate. The bottles are capped and pasteurized, the casks stoppered and distributed with no further treatment. Heather ale is produced in early June–early December; the cask-conditioned ale is available July–October; the bottled ale from July until early spring; the stronger Pictish Ale is made as a Christmas or New Year drink.

REGION OF PRODUCTION:
WEST SCOTLAND AND GENERAL SCOTLAND.

Mealie Pudding

DESCRIPTION:
A COOKED SUET AND CEREAL SAUSAGE IN SEVERAL SHAPES: A SINGLE LINK SAUSAGE, A SLICING SAUSAGE, A LARGE LINK SAUSAGE CURVED AND THE ENDS JOINED TO MAKE A LOOP, A BALL-LIKE HAGGIS SHAPE. WEIGHT: 125–250G. COLOUR: GREY. FLAVOUR: OATMEAL AND ONION, BUT DEPENDS LARGELY ON THE FLAVOUR OF THE SUET OR FAT.

HISTORY:
In the days before the turnip was used as winter feed for animals, Martinmas (11 November) was the time for killing the animals which could not be kept through the winter. 'Mairt' was an incredibly busy time and several families would join together to do the work. Every scrap of the beast was used –

the meat salted and puddings made from the innards. Mealie puddings (black and white) were made when beef cattle were killed. In the original communal system, oatmeal, onions and beef suet were mixed with salt and pepper in a large basin. Then blood was added to some of the mixture to make the 'bleedy' ones (black puddings). The intestines were thoroughly washed, usually in a burn, and then stuffed loosely with the mixture. They were tied up and boiled in a large pot.

The operation has now become almost completely commercial, carried out by either a butcher or meat-processing plant, though there are a few individuals who still make their own at home. They are consumed throughout the country. The pudding is sliced and fried with bacon and eggs; a whole pudding is cooked on top of a beef stew, or served as an accompaniment to meat or boiled potatoes; or they can be deep-fried and eaten with chips. They are also known as white pudding and, in Aberdeenshire as Jimmys while black puddings are known as Jocks. Without their skins, the mixture of oatmeal and onions is fried in a pan with fat and is known as 'skirlie' from the term 'skirl in the pan' meaning making a loud noise.

TECHNIQUE:

The 'Traditional Method' (McNeill, 1929): 'Toast two pounds of oatmeal in the oven, mix with it from a pound to a pound and a half of good beef suet and three or four fair-sized onions, all finely chopped. Add about a tablespoonful of salt and half that quantity of Jamaica pepper. Prepare your tripe skins as for Black Puddings and fill, not too full with the oatmeal mixture in the manner there indicated. Boil for an hour, pricking them occasionally with a fork to prevent them from bursting. These puddings will keep good for months if hung up and kept dry, or better, if kept buried in oatmeal in the girnel or meal chest.'

REGION OF PRODUCTION:

THROUGHOUT GENERAL SCOTLAND.

North Ronaldsay Sheep

DESCRIPTION:

SMALL, FINE-BONED ANIMALS, WITH DARK, TENDER, FINE-GRAINED, WELL-FLAVOURED AND SLIGHTLY GAMY FLESH. PRIMITIVE SHEEP HAVE A LOWER PROPORTION OF SATURATED FATTY ACIDS THAN COMMERCIAL BREEDS.

HISTORY:

North Ronaldsay sheep evolved in an oceanic climate, windy and wet but mild, thanks to the Gulf Stream. The Orkneys are flat and low-lying; the soil is good and much is cultivated or used as pasture for cattle and sheep, which are part of a subsistence economy known as crofting. This incorporates small-scale farming and cultivation of crops like potatoes and kale, backed up by fishing and cottage industries such as weaving or knitting. All the good land is used for crops and cattle; sheep are expected to live on the common, less fertile land, which in the Orkneys often means the foreshore surrounding habitable land.

The first recorded comments on the native sheep were in the early nineteenth century (*OED*). In 1861, Mrs Beeton remarked they were 'restless and unprofitable'. They may be considered as ancestors of the Shetlands which, together with other primitive breeds found on the Scottish islands, probably owe many of their characteristics to introductions by the Vikings. The sheep now survive only on a single inhabited island, North Ronaldsay, and on several small holms or uninhabited islands the most notable of which is Linga Holm – hence their other names of Holme sheep or Holmies. In the early nineteenth century, a wall was built around North Ronaldsay's agricultural acreage to exclude these near-feral sheep from more conventional grazing. They have since lived on the foreshore, surviving largely on seaweed. They are physiologically adapted to this diet, utilizing dietary copper very efficiently, even developing copper poisoning on richer grazing.

The ewes are brought into grass fields for a few weeks around lambing in May.

After long decline, the primitive breeds are now valuable for both genetic and commercial reasons. In the 1970s, fears for the health of this small population in so restricted an area led to the purchase of Linga Holm by the Rare Breeds Survival Trust who established and manage a flock there. There is a demand for their meat. However, the potential market is very distant, adding to difficulties and cost. Lamb from North Ronaldsay is available on the Orkneys and in a few specialist butchers on the mainland in late August and early September. Other lambs are raised on the Orkneys to a more settled agricultural pattern: these are Cheviots.

TECHNIQUE:

North Ronaldsay sheep are recognized to be exceptionally hardy and prolific. Meat from all the primitive breeds requires hanging for 7 days to develop optimum flavour and tenderness.

REGION OF PRODUCTION:

ORKNEY ISLANDS.

Red Deer Venison

A STAG WEIGHS APPROXIMATELY 105KG, HIND 70KG (CLEANED). THE MEAT IS DARK CRIMSON RED, CLOSE-GRAINED, WITH FIRM, WHITE FAT.

HISTORY:

The word venison formerly referred to the flesh of game in general. Now it is restricted to that of the various species of deer found in Britain. There is much early evidence for its use as food by the whole population. After 1066, first in England and later in Scotland, landowners became increasingly restrictive about hunting. In the Scottish Highlands, venison was caught and distributed through the clan, which shared equitably the produce of the land among its people. The deer were hunted by a method known as the tinchel (Annette Hope, *A Caledonian Feast*, 1987). This involved a large number of men moving herds from the hills over days, or weeks, into a funnel-like enclosure at the head of a glen. The deer were killed as they attempted to escape. The animals concerned would be red deer, as the woodland species live on lower ground. This method was used into the 1700s. Thereafter, as landowners claimed the Highlands for themselves, the meat only entered the diet of the poor when it was poached.

By the nineteenth century the range of red deer had become restricted to very specific areas of Britain, by far the most important was the Scottish Highlands. At this time, the art of stalking, still practised today, became important. The factors which led to its development were the retreat of the deer to remote and inaccessible areas; the depopulation of the Highlands, reducing the manpower available; the availability of improved firearms; and the need for Scottish landowners to earn money – which they did by creating shooting estates. In 1811 there were 6 of these in the Scottish Highlands; by 1842, there were 40.

The pattern thus set has never been completely reversed and venison remains a luxury meat. For a long period in the second half of the twentieth century a large percentage of Highland venison was exported, principally to Germany. But largely due to several companies' efforts to reverse this trend, as well as the production of a small amount of farmed venison's unique flavour and high-quality, lean meat is now gaining more local customers.

The history of English venison is not so very different from the experience of Scotland. The meat of the roe deer and other species has always been jealously reserved to those groups who have had the privilege of hunting it: at first the king, then his noble vassals, then land-owners whoever they may be. Venison entered the general diet through gift, not sale, unless it was poached (E. P. Thompson, *Whigs and Hunters*, 1975). Culinary treatment of the meat has been conservative, but with better hanging and butchering techniques, as well as more available information, it is being used in a more adventurous fashion.

TECHNIQUE:

The season in Scotland is 21 October–15 February for hinds; 1 July–20 October for stags.

After shooting, the deer are gralloched (innards removed) immediately. They are transported on hill-ponies to a collection point to be trucked in refrigerated vehicles to a production unit. Here they are skinned, inspected by a veterinary surgeon, hung for approximately 2–3 days and then butchered into prime cuts and other products such as sausages and mince.

REGION OF PRODUCTION:

SCOTLAND, HIGHLANDS.

Reestit Mutton

CURED MUTTON FROM VARIOUS CUTS. COLOUR: PALE CREAM
FAT, DEEP RED LEAN. FLAVOUR: SALTY, MATURE MUTTON.
TEXTURE: HARD, DRY.

HISTORY:

Reestit mutton originated in the need to preserve a surplus
through the winter. It was salted and dried by hanging from the
rafter (reestit) in a croft house with an open peat fire; photographs
from the early 1900s show the reestit mutton still hanging from
the roof frame though the fire has been transferred to a range
with a chimney. While Shetlanders continue to reest mutton at
home, some Lerwick butchers also cure the meat. An explana-
tory notice for visitors in a butcher's window is headed: 'Reestit
Mutton What is it? Traditionally, it was salted lamb or mutton
dried above a peat fire. It will keep for years if you keep it dry.
Reestit mutton soup is an acquired taste that you acquire at the
first taste. A small piece is enough to flavour a pot of soup
which should include cabbage, carrots, neeps and tatties.'

The meat is first used to make stock for broths, then taken
out and eaten separately with potatoes, or chopped finely and
returned to the broth. Alternatively, it can be eaten cold in a
Shetland bannock (made from wheat, not barley or oats), or
chopped finely and mixed into 'milgrew', a colloquial term for
milk gruel (porridge made with milk). Reestit mutton is an important feature of the festive food at the Up-Helly-Aa celebrations in January when platters of the best cuts are served with
bannocks, oatcakes and butter at *ceilidhs* after the ritual burning
of the Viking longboat.

TECHNIQUE:

The meat is cut up and put into a 'secret' brine recipe which
one butcher describes as approximately 80 per cent salt to
20 per cent sugar. It is left for 10–21 days, then hung on hooks

to dry. The recipe in *A Shetland Cookbook* (J. Simmonds, 1978) requires 'three and a half pounds (1.5kg) of salt; four quarts (4.5 litres) of water; six ounces (150g) of sugar; two to three ounces (50–75g) of saltpetre; about sixteen pounds (7.25kg) of mutton'.

REGION OF PRODUCTION:
SHETLAND.

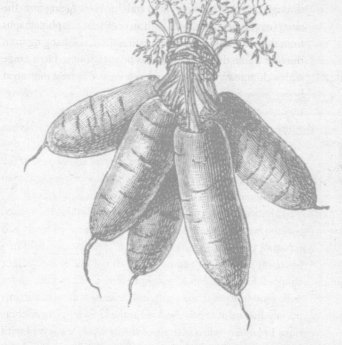

'I saw him even now going the way of all flesh, that is to say towards the kitchen.'

JOHN WEBSTER, *WESTWARD HOE*

This salt–sugar pickle is the old method for adding character to more mature mutton from native breeds such as the Blackface (Blackie). Reestit Mutton is a variation using native Shetland Sheep which is available from Shetland butchers where the joints are both pickled and then dried. Just as fish smokers in the early nineteenth century modified their smoking cures to produce a more lightly preserved fish, so an early method for mutton is modifed with shorter pickling times.

Catherine Brown

FROM *A YEAR IN A SCOTS KITCHEN*

PICKLE FOR 2–3KG/4LB 8OZ–6LB 12OZ LEG OF MUTTON

2L/3PT 10FLOZ WATER
600G/1LB 5OZ COARSE SEA SALT
250G/9OZ BROWN MUSCOVADO SUGAR
1 SPRIG OF BAY LEAVES
1 SPRIG THYME
5 CRUSHED JUNIPER BERRIES
5 CRUSHED PEPPERCORNS

to pickle:
Put the ingredients into a pan and bring to the boil. Stir to dissolve the salt and sugar and leave to simmer for about ten minutes. Leave to cool.

Put the cold pickle into an earthenware crock or plastic bucket with a lid. Immerse the meat and keep below the surface by laying a heavy plate on top. Cover and keep in a cool place.

Pickle time should be shorter if meat is thin and without bone, longer if it is thick and with bone. For a 3kg/6lb 12oz leg of mutton between twelve and twenty-four hours will produce a well-flavoured result. The longer it is left in the pickle the stronger it becomes.

If kept in a cool dark place, the pickle mixture will keep for several months and can be used again.

to cook the meat:
Rinse under cold water; put into a large pot with three medium onions stuck with three cloves; a sprig of bay leaves; eight peppercorns; three carrots peeled and chopped in two; a small turnip, peeled and chopped roughly in large pieces. Cover with cold water and simmer very gently till the meat is tender. Remove and serve hot with boiled floury potatoes or cold with oatcakes and butter. Use the cooking liquor to make broth. Check first for saltiness and adjust by adding water if necessary. Some of the less choice cuts of meat can be chopped and added to the broth.

Note: This pickle can also be used for pork, duck and chicken.

Rowan Jelly

DESCRIPTION:

THIS IS CRIMSON RED WITH A SWEET-ASTRINGENT FLAVOUR. OTHER FRUIT PRODUCE DIFFERENT COLOURS: SLOE, DARK PURPLE; HAWTHORN, PALE RUBY RED; WILD CHERRY, DARK RUBY RED; BRAMBLE, BLACKISH-PURPLE.

HISTORY:

The jelly from wild Highland berries was originally used as a reviving drink – a spoonful mixed with boiling water, whisky or rum – or as a sweet pudding with cream. The drink is mentioned by St Fond (1784) in his account of travels in the Hebrides. A description of jellies with cream as a dessert appears in an account by young Elizabeth Grant of Rothimurchus when visiting a relative in 1812. Inside her hostess's deep-shelved pantry, beside the butter, honey, sweetmeats and spiced whisky, were pots of preserved jellies. The cook skimmed some cream off the milk, emptied the whole pot of jelly on a plate and poured over the cream. The dish, she explains, was known as 'bainne briste' meaning broken milk.

Several companies make rowan jelly but the pioneer of preserves from wild fruits has been Phillipa Fraser, of Moniack Wineries, who started collecting berries as a consequence of country wine-making.

TECHNIQUE:

The berries are gathered, beginning in late summer with wild cherries and running through to late autumn for rowan and sloes. After cleaning, they are boiled with apples (which contribute pectin) in water to produce a juice; this is strained and boiled with sugar until setting point is reached. Commonly there are 60g berries per 100g of jelly. Total sugar content is 60g per 100g.

REGION OF PRODUCTION:

NORTH SCOTLAND.

Shetland Sassermeat

DESCRIPTION:

A MIXTURE OF RAW, SALTED AND SPICED BEEF, EITHER MOULDED INTO 'SQUARE' SAUSAGES (IN A TIN OF THE TYPE USED FOR LORNE SAUSAGES) WHICH PRODUCES A SLICE APPROXIMATELY 10CM SQUARE AND 1CM THICK, OR SOLD UNSHAPED BY WEIGHT.

HISTORY:

Links with Scandinavia (Shetland was once part of Norway) and the need for a method of preservation that would last through lengthy northern winters have created a number of original Shetland cures for meat and fish. Unlike reestit mutton (which retains its original form), sassermeat, also known as saucermeat, has been modified and is not now intended to last the winter through.

It used to be heavily salted and spiced. Crofters would make a winter's supply all at once and store it in an earthenware crock for use as required. It would be mixed with onions and either fresh meat or bread crumbs, then bound with egg or milk to make fried patties ('bronies') or a baked loaf. Though some traditionalists continue to make their own, most sassermeat is now made by butchers in a milder form.

TECHNIQUE:

Beef and fat are minced together and mixed with rusk, water, salt and a spicing mixture. Each butcher uses a different seasoning and regards his particular formula as a trade secret. Proportions quoted in *A Shetland Cookbook* are 3kg meat and 100g salt mixed with 1 teaspoon each of allspice, black pepper, white pepper, and ground cloves, and half a teaspoon of cinnamon. This can be pressed by hand into a Lorne sausage tin to make a loaf 38cm by 10cm, with sloping sides, weighing about 2kg. The sausage is turned out of this mould and left to set and harden in the refrigerator for several hours before slicing to order.

REGION OF PRODUCTION:

SHETLAND.

Shetland Sheep

DESCRIPTION:

SHETLANDS ARE SMALL AND FINE-BONED; THE NATIONAL SHEEP ASSOCIATION COMMENTS THAT THE HILL-BRED WETHER MUTTON 'IS CLAIMED TO BE UNSURPASSABLE'. MEAT IS GENERALLY TENDER, FINE-GRAINED, WELL-FLAVOURED AND SLIGHTLY GAMY, A WELL-FATTENED PRIME LAMB YIELDING A CARCASS OF 11–12KG, ALTHOUGH SOME AS LITTLE AS 8KG. THEY HAVE A LOW PERCENTAGE OF SATURATED FATTY ACIDS.

HISTORY:

Shetlands have long been valued both for meat and for their very fine wool, coloured from white to dark brown. They are the foundation of an important textile industry on the islands. The wool is comparable in fineness to the Merino's and its worth was early recognized by those anxious to encourage domestic resources and manufacture. Shetlands are one of the Scottish primitives. Several are known on the islands, such as the North Ronaldsay. At first, they were spread through the whole of northern Scotland, only dying out on the mainland in the 1880s due to constant cross-breeding, especially with the Cheviot, to develop a more meaty conformation while retaining something of the quality of the wool.

The Shetland Flock Book Society was founded in 1927. After a long period of decline, the primitives are now thought valuable for genetic and commercial reasons. It was never in doubt that it would survive on the islands themselves, but its worth as a grazer of marginal lands has made it among the most popular of British rare breeds. The pure-bred stock remains for breeding but is still much crossed with Cheviots for meat, and has now been awarded Protected Designation of Origin (PDO).

TECHNIQUE:

Shetland sheep are kept on common grazings, where they take care of themselves for much of the year. The breed is hardy and easy to lamb; it is also naturally short-tailed and resistant to foot-rot. Although these breeds are shorn in conventional husbandry systems, they will shed their fleeces naturally in summer if left alone. Excess lambs culled from these flocks in the late summer are used for meat, but some breeding according to the stratified system of production also goes on, in which a first-cross generation is produced using Cheviots. In turn, these are crossed with Suffolks, to give lambs intended solely as meat for the mainland. These crossbred animals are kept on the inbye land. The National Sheep Association remarks, 'It is unlikely that it will ever be supplanted in its native area where the breed will remain as a pure bred stock under the harsher hill conditions, or as a parent stock for the production of cross ewes and lambs under more kindly conditions.'

REGION OF PRODUCTION:

SCOTLAND, SHETLAND ISLANDS.

Spoot

DESCRIPTION:

A BIVALVE; THE NARROW SHELL CAN BE UP TO 12CM LONG BUT
IS ONLY 1.5–2CM WIDE; IT IS STRAIGHT, AND SLIGHTLY GREEN-
BROWN IN COLOUR. THE MEAT IS TRANSLUCENT WHITE,
COARSELY TEXTURED, WITH AN EXCELLENT SEA FLAVOUR.
IF OVERCOOKED, IT BECOMES CHEWY AND INEDIBLE.

HISTORY:

Spoots is the name in Orcadian dialect for *Ensis ensis*, the razor-
shell clam. These are not eaten in the British Isles except by the
inhabitants of some Scottish islands, who regard them as a
delicacy. They form part of an ancient gathering tradition in an
area in which food was often in short supply and all available
edible items found use sooner or later. The Orkney Islands
exhibit the strongest appetite for these fish. It is not clear for
how many centuries they have been considered a local delicacy:
the name spoots was noted by the beginning of the 1800s
(*OED*).

The Moray Firth, a little further south, also yields spoots.
Dived and dredged spoots are available October–May; hand-
fishing takes place principally in March and September, when
the equinox produces low ebb tides.

In the Orkneys, spoots are eaten for any main meal. They are
taken plain, straight from the opened shell, or turned briefly in
melted butter.

TECHNIQUE:

Spoots are renowned for being difficult to catch. They are found
in wet sand, and are only exposed at very low ebb tides. The
method for spooting is to walk backwards along the beach,
watching for the little spoot (spout) of water ejected by these
creatures, which lie concealed just below the surface. If one is
located, the spooter inserts a knife into the sand to locate the
shell and then twists it round very quickly to bring it to the

surface. This requires practice and skill for if the spoots sense danger they burrow quickly downwards beyond reach. On some beaches, it is claimed that they can be brought to the surface by pouring a small quantity of dry salt into the hole on the surface, but mixed reports about the effectiveness of the technique are given by those who have tried. Modern methods in commercial use are diving (which also requires skill, as it too involves problems locating and catching the fish) and suction dredging, which is the easiest but the most capital-intensive method.

If desired, the fish can be left in sea water overnight to cleanse them. As spoots have shells which are permanently open at both ends, the risk of contamination is too great to allow them to be marketed alive like other bivalves; this may account for their localized popularity. Spoots are opened just before eating by placing the shellfish on a hot griddle and removing the meat as soon as the shells open. Or they can be placed in boiling water. The stomach bag can be cut away before consumption.

Although these clams are found on English beaches, they have not been gathered with any great gastronomic enthusiasm. An episode on the beaches of south Devon in 1998 left 200 holiday-makers lacerated on the feet by the (razor) sharp shells (hence the English name) that were unexpectedly exposed on the surface by abnormally low tides. No mention in news reports was made of their palatability, only their capacity to wound.

REGION OF PRODUCTION:
THROUGHOUT GENERAL SCOTLAND, HIGHLANDS AND ORKNEYS.

Scotland: Countrywide

Clootie Dumpling

DESCRIPTION:

A PUDDING STEAMED IN A CLOTH (CLOOT) – A ROUND, FLAT-
TENED BALL-LIKE SHAPE, MORE CURVED AND ROUNDED ON
THE UPPER SIDE WITH A SHINY LEATHER-LIKE SKIN, OFTEN
SOLD CUT IN SLICES. A WHOLE DUMPLING WEIGHS APPROXI-
MATELY 900G (LARGE), 680G (MEDIUM), OR 113G (SMALL).
COLOUR: LIGHT BROWN ON OUTSIDE, DARKER INSIDE, DEPTH
OF COLOUR DEPENDS ON AMOUNT OF SPICES AND BLACK
TREACLE. FLAVOUR AND TEXTURE: SPICY, SWEET, FRUITY.

HISTORY:

This pudding developed as a sweet version of the savoury pudding (haggis) stuffed into sheep's or pig's stomach bags and
boiled in a large cauldron. Using instead a cotton or linen cloth,
the sweet pudding mixture was made originally as the Scottish
alternative to a baked celebration fruit cake for holidays, birth-
days and during winter solstice celebrations, known in Scotland
as the Daft Days.

Easily made in the common domestic setting where there was
no oven and the cooking was done solely over a fire in a large
pot, these special-occasion dumplings usually contained a selec-
tion of 'surprises': a ring signifying marriage, a coin – wealth, a
button – bachelorhood, a thimble – spinsterhood, a wishbone –
the heart's desire, a horse-shoe – good luck. Compared with rich
celebration fruit cakes, or an English Christmas pudding, the
dumpling mixture is much plainer. No hard and fast rules apply
to the degree of richness, or even to the exact content since it has
always been a rule-of-thumb affair, depending largely on the fortunes of the family.

Clootie dumpling is served with custard, cream or a bowl of

soft brown sugar. When cold it is often fried with bacon and eggs for breakfast. Unlike Christmas pudding tradition south of the border it does not have the same strict linkage to midwinter feasting.

TECHNIQUE:

A typical recipe is 125g self-raising flour, 175g fine white breadcrumbs, 125g beef suet, 2 teaspoons baking powder, 2 teaspoons each of freshly ground cinnamon, ginger and nutmeg, 175g sultanas, 175g California raisins, 2 tablespoons Golden Syrup, 2 tablespoons black treacle, 2 eggs, 1 large cooking apple, grated, 1 large carrot, grated, and milk to mix. Use a cotton or linen cloth 550mm square. To prepare the pot and cloth, fill a large pot with water, place a metal grid or upside-down saucer in the base. Bring to the boil and put in the cloth for a few minutes. Lift out with tongs and spread on a table. Sprinkle with plain flour, shake off excess. Put all the ingredients into a large bowl (add trinkets wrapped in greaseproof paper) and mix to a fairly stiff consistency with orange juice. Put in the centre of the cloth, bring up edges and tie with string, leaving space for expansion. Hold up the tied ends and pat the dumpling into a good round shape. Place in simmering water which should come about halfway up the dumpling, and simmer for 4 hours. Fill a large bowl with cold water. Lift out the dumpling and plunge into the cold water. Keep submerged for about a minute and this will release the cloth from the pudding skin. Put into a bowl about the same size as the dumpling, untie the string, open out the cloth, place the serving-dish on top and reverse. Peel off the cloth and dry out the outer 'skin' in a warm place. Serve with sweetened double cream.

REGION OF PRODUCTION:
SCOTLAND.

Crowdie Cheese

DESCRIPTION:

PASTEURIZED, SOFT COW'S MILK CHEESE. THERE ARE SOME VARIANTS. GRUTH DHU (BLACK CROWDIE): CROWDIE MIXED WITH DOUBLE CREAM AND ROLLED IN TOASTED OATMEAL AND BLACK PEPPER. HRAMSA: CROWDIE MIXED WITH WILD GARLIC AND WHITE AND RED PEPPER. GALIC HRAMSA: ROLLED IN CRUMBLED FLAKED HAZELNUTS AND ALMONDS. CROWDIE IS SOLD IN PLASTIC TUBS OF APPROXIMATELY 150G; GRUTH DHU IN CYLINDRICAL ROLLS OF APPROXIMATELY 125G, UP TO 1KG; HRAMSA AND GALIC IN ROLLS OF 125G; HIGHLAND SOFT IN TUBS OF 150G. COLOUR: CREAM OR WHITE. FLAVOUR: SHARP, ACIDIC, REFRESHING.

HISTORY:

Crowdie was at one time the universal breakfast dish of Scotland. In the seventeenth century the name was applied to foods akin to porridge – mixtures of oatmeal and water which had a slightly curdled texture (*OED*). There were various developments of this in the Lowlands but in the Highlands, by the nineteenth century, the word had come to denote a species of milk curd.

Today, the Lowland meaning has been replaced entirely and crowdie has become known solely as the Highlanders' soft cheese. It is of ancient origin, probably having roots in Pictish or Viking practices, and linked to a system of transhumance, in which cattle, sheep and goats were taken to mountain pastures and the milk made into butter and cheese. Surplus crowdie was mixed with butter, packed in earthenware crocks, then covered with a sealing layer of melted butter. These were kept in a cool barn for use through the winter. This was known as crowdie-butter.

This butter and the way of life that engendered it were stopped by the Highland Clearances. The commercial revival of the soft crowdie is almost entirely due to the pioneering efforts of Susanna Stone and her late husband Reggie, who started making it for sale in the early 1960s. They were post-war revivalist farmhouse cheese-makers who in the early days battled against bureaucracy to produce the native cheese. 'The great treat,' said G.W. Lockhart in *The Scot and his Oats* (1983), 'was to have crowdie mixed with fresh cream and piled on an oatcake with fresh salted butter. Then you had a royal feast of flavours – acid, sweet and salt, and better perhaps, a royal mixture of textures, soft, crisp and crunchy.'

TECHNIQUE:

The traditional croft method, described by Susanna Stone as made by her mother, was to leave the bowl of milk at the fireside in winter or in a warm place in summer. It soured naturally and formed a curd. The curds were cooked lightly, until they scrambled (the curd and whey separated). The curds were poured into a muslin-lined bowl and the ends of the muslin were drawn together and tied with string. The bag was hung from a branch of a tree for a few days to drip, or over the tap in the sink, until most of the whey drained out.

The modern method, made by Susanna Stone, follows the old by souring the milk with a starter and allowing it to curd without rennet. The scrambling procedure is followed and the curd is hung in muslin bags to drain. Others now make crowdie, though not all in the old way without rennet. Flavourings are added by some brands to suit the modern palate.

REGION OF PRODUCTION:

NORTH SCOTLAND AND GENERAL SCOTLAND.

'Floury' Potatoes

DESCRIPTION:

ROUND OR OVAL-SHAPED, FIRM TUBERS OF VARYING SIZES AND WEIGHTS. THE 2 MOST COMMON VARIETIES ARE: GOLDEN WONDER, WITH A RUSSET SKIN AND WHITE FLESH, A STRONG FLAVOUR AND ELONGATED PEAR-SHAPE; KERR'S PINK, WHICH HAS A PARTLY PINK SKIN, CREAM FLESH, A DISTINCTIVE FLAVOUR, AND IS A ROUND SHAPE.

HISTORY:

By the nineteenth century, farm carts selling 'mealy tatties' (dry floury potatoes boiled in salted water) had become a common sight on the streets of Scottish cities. This type of potato, favoured by the Scots, has a dry, powdery surface when cooked, and a stronger, more dominant flavour than most available in the British market. Potatoes had been gradually accepted in Scotland during the late eighteenth and early nineteenth centuries, especially in areas of impoverished peasantry. The crop became very important in the West and the Islands. *An Account of the Economic History of the Hebrides and Highlands* (1808) states that by about 1763 the people were subsisting on potatoes for 9 months of the year. Potatoes also combined well with the northern Scots' staple diet of milk and fish. 'Fish with oat bread or potatoes, without any accompaniment at all, forms the three daily meals of the Shetland cottager,' said E. Edmondston, in *Sketches and Tales of the Shetland Isles* (1856). Annette Hope (1987) cites numerous references to illustrate the importance of potatoes to the inhabitants of western and northern Scotland. Both she and Jeremy Cherfas ('Vanishing Potatoes, not an illusion', 1995) comment on regional preferences for floury varieties which exist in western Scotland down to the present day.

Many floury varieties have been raised, including Dunbar Rover, Arran Victory, Duke of York and Champion as well as

Golden Wonder and Kerr's Pink. Golden Wonder was raised in 1906 by John Brown near Arbroath; it remains one of the varieties with the highest amount of dry matter. Kerr's Pink was raised by James Henry in 1907 and was originally known as Henry's Seedling until it won the Lord Derby Gold Medal at the Ormskirk Trials in 1916. Its merits were recognized by a seedsman (Mr Kerr) who bought the seed and renamed it in 1917.

TECHNIQUE:

Growing underground, potatoes have an advantage over grain crops in a climate which tends towards high rainfall and strong winds; and the rain and cool temperatures also suit the crop. Potatoes flourish in the poor soils of the Scottish Highlands, although for commercial growth, areas of flatter land are favoured – in Ayrshire, on the West coast, and in the fertile soils of East and Central Scotland from Aberdeenshire to the Borders. In the nineteenth century, potatoes were cultivated on a system of hand-dug furrows known as 'lazy beds', whose remains can be seen in many remote parts of the West Highlands. Cultivation is now mechanized. The Scots have particular expertise in the development of new potato varieties, originally derived from the realisation that potato blight would otherwise seriously affect the crop.

March is the main month for early potato planting, April for maincrop. Disease-free seed potatoes are planted in drills in clod-free soils. Harvesting starts in September and is mostly mechanized. All potatoes are lifted by the end of October. They may be sold immediately or treated with sprout-suppressants and fungicides and stored in cool conditions excluding light. Though neither Golden Wonder nor Kerr's Pink are grown on a large scale, the demand remains. Recently, increased interest in potato varieties has led to more attention to their qualities.

REGION OF PRODUCTION:
SCOTLAND.

Haggis

DESCRIPTION:

A COOKED PUDDING OF SHEEP'S PLUCK IN A SHEEP'S STOMACH BAG: THE SHAPE AN OVAL MISSHAPEN BALL. WEIGHT: FROM 75–100G (INDIVIDUAL SIZE) TO 4–5KG ('CHIEFTAIN' HAGGIS TO FEED 20); THE MEAN IS 250–500G. COLOUR: GREYISH-CREAM. FLAVOUR: PEPPERY, SOMETIMES WITH A STRONG LIVER TASTE.

HISTORY:

Though the habit of cooking the entrails of an animal stuffed into the stomach bag has an ancient ancestry, at least as far back as Roman cookery, the haggis's development in Britain has taken some curious twists. The word itself is English, not exclusively Scottish, its derivation unknown. There are plenty of medieval and early-modern English references to establish it was a dish eaten throughout Britain – especially in the highland zones where oatmeal was an acceptable grain. It was not always made with sheep's pluck. Calf and pig are mentioned by Gervase Markham (*The English Hus-wife*, 1615). Robert May (*The Accomplisht Cook*, 1660) devotes a section to 'Sheeps Haggas Puddings', and includes a fast-day version as well as one made with calf's paunch and innards. The dish also figures in much later English dialect glossaries, for example from Northumberland and Gloucestershire, but at some point in the eighteenth century, it begins to be perceived as specifically Caledonian. Hannah Glasse (*The Art of Cookery Made Plain and Easy*, 1747) refers to 'Scotch haggass' (although suggesting it be made with calf's pluck) and Smollett writes in *Humphrey Clinker* (1771), 'I am not yet Scotchman enough to relish their singed sheep's-head and haggice.'

Around this time, Scotland's poet Robert Burns wrote his 'Address to a Haggis'. Drawing attention to the charms and usefulness of bringing together the odds and ends of offal in an economical 'Great Chieftain o' the Puddin race', he turned the humble haggis into a symbol of Scottish sense of worth. After his death in 1796, the Edinburgh literati honoured his memory with a supper where the haggis was piped in by a piper and addressed with Burns' poem in a ritual procedure. Burns' Suppers have continued to be celebrated every year around 25 January, the poet's birthday, and the haggis has become inextricably linked with Scotland and Burns. Today it is made by all Scottish butchers and several meat-processing companies to meet a year-round demand.

The ingredients have varied over the years. Fifteenth-century recipes use the liver and blood of the sheep, while later, in the 1600s, a meatless 'Haggas Pudding in a Sheep's Paunch' requires a highly seasoned mixture of oatmeal, beef suet, and onions; it was sewn up and boiled, and served after cutting a hole in the top to be filled with butter melted with two eggs. Another recipe uses a calf's paunch and entrails, minced with bread, egg yolks, cream, spices, dried fruits and herbs, served as a sweet with sugar and almonds. Meg Dods (1826) has what she calls a finer haggis, 'made by parboiling and skinning sheep's tongues and kidneys, and substituting these minced, for most of the lights [lungs], and soaked bread or crisped crumbs for the toasted meal [oatmeal]'.

Among professional haggis-makers there is some controversy about the correct ingredients, since not all use a sheep's pluck of liver, heart and lights (lungs) but add other meats, or pig or ox liver – deemed by purists to produce a haggis without the real 'haggis-flavour'. These recipes are closely guarded secrets. The recent winner of a competition remarked that his had come from an old butcher he had worked for who had only relinquished his recipe under pressure when on the point of retirement.

Haggis may be served in its skin with mashed potatoes and mashed turnip ('tatties and neeps'), or with clapshot (mashed potatoes and turnip mixed together). To reheat, it should be wrapped in foil and baked in the oven. 'Haggis meat,' said Meg Dods, 'for those who do not admire the natural shape, may be poured out of the bag, and served in a deep dish.' It may also be made in a long sausage shape, sliced and fried or grilled.

Haggis is made by many craft butchers and several larger companies. It is sent through the mails to expatriate Scots throughout the world.

TECHNIQUE:

The pluck or innards (liver, heart and lungs) are washed and put to boil until tender. When cool, the meat is chopped or minced finely and mixed with oatmeal (which may be pinhead, coarse or medium), onions, salt, pepper and spices. It is again put through a coarser mincer. The mixture is moistened, usually with meat gravy, and pumped into prepared natural or artificial casings which are then sealed. The haggis is boiled in water for about an hour, depending on size. The filling is always rather loose as it swells up to fill the skins during boiling.

REGION OF PRODUCTION:

SCOTLAND.

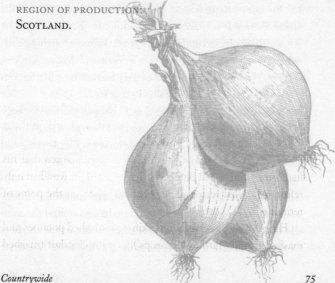

Heather Honey

DESCRIPTION:

THIS IS SELDOM SOLD AS SINGLE-HEATHER HONEY, BUT LING
HEATHER HONEY CAN BE DISTINGUISHED FROM THE OTHERS
BY ITS THICK, JELLY-LIKE (THIXOTROPIC) CONSISTENCY WITH
A STRONG AROMA AND FLAVOUR. HONEY FROM BELL HEATHER
IS THINNER, WITH A MORE BITTER EDGE, WHILE CROSS-
LEAVED GIVES A THIN HONEY WITH LIGHTER FLAVOUR.

HISTORY:

Honey as a sweetener in the Scottish diet combines particularly
well with the distinctive flavours of oatmeal and whisky in a
number of drinks and dishes. Originally it was collected from
wild colonies of bees: 'The boys,' says Osgood Mackenzie in
A Hundred Years in the Highlands (1921), 'were able to collect
large quantities of wild honey, which, by applying heat to it, was
run into glass bottles and sold at the Stornoway markets. Hunting for wild-bee nests was one of the great ploys for the boys in
the autumn … Cameron tells me that, as a young boy, before he
left his home, there was an island in Loch Bhacha Chreamha
where there was no necessity for hunting for bees' nests, as the
whole island seemed under bees, the nests almost touching each
other in the moss at the roots of tall heather … My stalker, too,
informs me that his home at Kernsary used to be quite famous
for its wild bees, but they finally disappeared.'

Beekeeping, which originated as a hobby or sideline for people running other businesses, continues to attract an enthusias-
tic following. The flavour of heather honey is highly esteemed
for its distinctive character.

TECHNIQUE:

To ensure purity, hives are filled with unused combs and 'flitted'
each summer, as the heather comes into bloom around the middle of July, to positions on the heather moors where the bees
can collect the maximum nectar in the shortest time. To extract

the honey, the outer caps are shaved off and the combs subjected to a Honey Loosener (nylon needles with a bulbous end which disturbs the honey). The combs are then put into a Tangential Swinging Basket Reversible which extracts by alternating 2 slow swinging movements with 2 fast. The honey is sieved into barrels and seeded (mixed with about a tenth volume of honey of the correct texture from the previous year's harvest) before it is poured into jars. Combs are cut and boxed.

PRODUCTION:
An average amount of honey per hive can vary from 350g to 69kg with the average working out at 23–30kg. A medium to large producer will have 300–400 hives.

REGION OF PRODUCTION:
SCOTLAND.

Highland Cattle

DESCRIPTION:
AVERAGE DRESSED CARCASS WEIGHT FOR 26-MONTH STEER, 280KG. FLESH DARK RED, MARBLED WITH INTRA-MUSCULAR CREAM FAT; LEAN EXTERNAL FAT. DEEP-FLAVOURED MEAT BECAUSE OF MATURITY; AT ITS BEST WHEN IT HAS BEEN HUNG 2–3 WEEKS.

HISTORY:
Before the Jacobite Rebellion of 1745, native Highland cattle were an important part of the clan-based economy. Used as a supply of milk, cheese and butter, the dairy cows were driven in the summer months to the mountain pastures. The women and children of the clan moved with them to live in sheilings (dwellings in the hills). While the women made cheese and butter, men herded the surplus cattle south along ancient drove roads to markets in Falkirk and Crieff where they were bought by graziers for finishing on more lush lowland pastures.

By the mid-nineteenth century the trade had reduced, partly on the break-up of the clan system following the Highland Clearances, partly because of demand for better quality beef. Those early cattle were often 4–5 years old, their carcasses did not provide the same tender meat as young beasts reared and fattened nearer the market on the new fodder crops.

Although in commercial decline, the breed was encouraged by certain lairds, notably the Stewart brothers of Harris, McNeil of Bara, and the Dukes of Hamilton and Argyll. Stock was selected from island and Highland populations, with no evidence of lowland blood. The breed society was founded in 1884 with 516 bulls listed in the first herd book. Most were black or dun. Some exports went to Canada in 1882 and, in the 1920s, more were made to the USA and South America. Now there has been a revival of interest, particularly for the quality of the lean meat. Butchers who specialize in pure Highland beef attract a loyal following.

TECHNIQUE:

Hardiness has remained a key characteristic of this breed. Like the Aberdeen-Angus, it is related to the Galloway. There is a common ancestry of primitive native stock. The Highland can survive well on rough mountain pasture with some additional feeding in winter. Because of their hardiness and very long, thick coats they withstand extreme cold and thrive outside during the winter.

REGION OF PRODUCTION:
SCOTLAND.

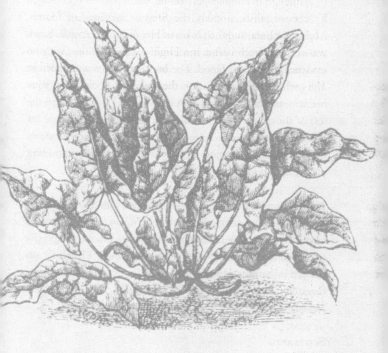

*'Better is a dinner of herbs where love is,
than a stalled ox and hatred therewith.'*

<small>PROVERBS, 15:17</small>

Lorne Sausage

DESCRIPTION:
AN UNCASED, UNCOOKED, FRESH BEEF SAUSAGE WITH A
SQUARE SECTION. CUT FROM A LARGE BLOCK AND SOLD IN
SLICES APPROXIMATELY 10CM SQUARE, 1CM THICK. COLOUR:
PINK. FLAVOUR: BEEF.

HISTORY:
This became associated in Glasgow with the comedian Tommy
Lorne, a popular music-hall performer of the decades between
the world wars who often made rude jokes about the Glasgow
square sausage describing it as a 'doormat'. It was an important
part of the urban eating habits of industrialized Scotland but remains popular. Known only in Glasgow as a Lorne sausage, the
rest of the country refers to it as a square or sliced sausage. Its
square, flat shape is a convenient fit for a morning roll along
with a fried egg. The use of beef reflects the less prominent
place that pig meat has in Scottish food habits.

TECHNIQUE:
Beef and fat in equal quantities are minced together and mixed
with binder, seasonings and water. The mixture is then pressed
into a Lorne tin (38cm long by 10cm at the top edge, tapering
to 8cm at the base and holding 2kg of mixture). The surface is
pressed by hand and the tin inverted on a tray immediately and
the sausage turned out. It is left to set and harden in the refrigerator for several hours before slicing to order.

REGION OF PRODUCTION:
SCOTLAND.

Malt Whisky

DESCRIPTION:

MALT WHISKY HAS SPECIFIC, SOMETIMES VERY PRONOUNCED, FLAVOURS AND AROMAS WHICH COME FROM A NUMBER OF FACTORS: THE QUALITY OF THE WATER, THE MALTED BARLEY, THE AMOUNT OF PEAT USED IN DRYING THE GRAIN, THE SHAPE OF THE POT STILL, THE TYPE OF WOOD IN WHICH IT MATURES, THE LENGTH OF TIME IT HAS MATURED AND THE TEMPERATURE AND HUMIDITY CONDITIONS DURING MATURATION. THE RANGE OF CHARACTER GOES FROM DEEP, PUNGENT, SMOKY AND EARTHY TO LIGHT, SUBTLE, GENTLE AND SWEET. COLOUR IS PALE STRAW TO DEEP GOLD. MALT IS AROUND 40 PER CENT PROOF.

DISTINCTION IS MADE BETWEEN HIGHLAND AND LOWLAND MALTS. THE DIVIDING LINE IS THE HIGHLAND BOUNDARY FAULT WHICH RUNS FROM THE FIRTH OF CLYDE IN THE WEST TO THE FIRTH OF TAY. IN THE HIGHLAND AREA THERE ARE FURTHER DIFFERENCES: SPEYSIDERS HAVE THEIR MELLOW, MALTY SWEETNESS; CAMPBELTOWN'S LIGHTLY PEATY MELLOWNESS COMPARES WITH ISLAY'S NOTABLY STRONGER PEATY FLAVOURS; NORTH HIGHLAND MALTS FROM INVERNESS TO WICK HAVE A DRY FRUITY-SWEETNESS, NOT NOTICEABLY PEATY; THE SOUTHERN MALTS NEAR PERTHSHIRE AND TO THE WEST ARE SOFT, LIGHT IN CHARACTER, OFTEN SWEET BUT SOME QUITE DRY; THE SMALL NUMBER OF WEST HIGHLAND MALTS BETWEEN OBAN AND FORT WILLIAM ARE SMOOTH AND ROUNDED; THE EASTERN HIGHLAND MALTS ALONG THE NORTH SEA COAST FROM BRECHIN TO BANFF HAVE A WIDE RANGE OF STYLES FROM FRUITY-SWEET TO PEATY-DRY; THE ISLAND MALTS OF JURA, MULL, SKYE AND ORKNEY (EXCLUDING ISLAY) HAVE A WIDE RANGE FROM DRY TO FULL, SWEET AND MALTY. LOWLAND MALTS ARE GENERALLY LESS ASSERTIVE; SOFT, LIGHT WITH A GENTLE SWEETNESS.

In describing a bottle, the term single malt indicates whisky produced by an individual distillery, while vatted malt is a blend from 2 or more.

HISTORY:

The Scots word whisky derives from the Gaelic *uisge beatha* meaning water of life – in Latin *aqua vitae* – the common European root words for distilled spirit. While its origins in Scotland are hazy, its fortunes have had some dramatic ups and downs since the first written reference in 1494 in the Scottish Exchequer Rolls as a commercial product made in monasteries: 'eight bolls of malt to Friar John Cor wherewith to make aquavitae.'

The particular connection of malt whisky with the Highlands was a result of enthusiasm for home distilling, to use surplus barley and produce a warming drink against a cold, inhospitable climate. It was drunk with meals at least 3 times a day and commonly given as a restorative to children.

In every Highland glen sacks of barley would be soaked in water, possibly in the burn, for a few days to soften the grain and begin germination. Then the grain would be spread to allow it to sprout, halted by drying over a peat fire. The malted grain would then go into a large tub with boiling water and yeast to ferment. Once fermented, it would be passed twice through the pot still and the middle cut (the drinkable part, without the dangerous methyl alcohols) would be separated from the foreshots and the aftercuts or feints. It was a skilled operation which produced a liquor strongly influenced by the local water and peat and much more highly esteemed than anything distilled in the Lowlands. The Highlanders' distilling activities grew and developed until the Union in 1707 when the government began to tax them. For over 100 years, until the Excise Act in 1823, the Highlanders smuggled their malted whisky illicitly with great ingenuity. But the passing of the act signalled the beginning of a new era of development and success for the Highlanders' malt whisky as old smugglers became legitimate and linked their considerable skills to the business of large-scale production.

For the rest of the century and until about the 1920s the malt distilleries flourished. The First World War, prohibition in America and then the Second World War and its aftermath, meant a slump which lasted until the 1950s. Thereafter, an export-led recovery was under way. New distilleries were built in the 1960s, old ones reopened and the production of malt whisky quadrupled in a decade. This upturn in fortunes has, on the whole, continued, with an emphasis on quality and individual character as the range and variety of distinctive malts has become more widely appreciated.

TECHNIQUE

The barley is soaked, spread out on the malting floor and turned daily until it sprouts. Germination is stopped by drying over a peat fire in a malt kiln. It is milled roughly and put into a mash tun and mixed with hot water until its sugars are dissolved producing a wort, when the solid remains of the barley are removed. The wort is cooled and mixed with yeast which converts it in about 2 days to a low-strength, alcoholic liquor known as the wash. This passes through first the wash still and then the spirit still, the middle cut is separated from the feints and foreshots and the spirit transferred to a vat to be mixed with water before transferring to casks where it must mature for 3 years before sale. Most will mature 8–15 years.

REGION OF PRODUCTION:
SCOTLAND.

Oatmeal

COMPOSITION: WHOLE OATS, LESS THE HUSK. COLOUR: GREYISH-BEIGE. FLAVOUR: SWEET-MEALY, THIS DEPENDS ON THE MOISTURE AND OIL CONTENT, DETERMINED BY THE VARIETY, THE DISTRICT WHERE IT IS GROWN, THE SOIL AND THE CLIMATE.

HISTORY:

It is not known where or when cultivated oats originated. The first evidence of the grain in Scotland is carbonized grain found at archaeological excavations along the Forth and Clyde Canal dated to approximately 100 BC. It is generally agreed that although oats thrive best in cool climates, they originally came from some warmer country to the east. In a climate such as Scotland's, growth is comparatively slow which allows the kernels to fill out and mature better.

Oats became the most important food grain in Scotland towards the end of the seventeenth century when they displaced barley. Oatmeal was more versatile and was generally better liked for its flavour when made into oatcakes, porridge and brose, the staple items of the peasant diet. By the end of the eighteenth century oatmeal had become firmly established as the people's grain. 'Oatmeal with milk, which they cook in different ways, is their constant food, three times a day, throughout the year, Sundays and holidays included,' says Donaldson in *A General View of Agriculture of the Carse of Gowrie* (1794). Throughout the nineteenth century its popularity continued to increase. The figure of the penniless Scottish university scholar, surviving on his sack of oatmeal, is legendary. The mid-term holiday known as 'Meal Monday' was given to allow the student to return home to replenish his supply of oatmeal.

With the industrial revolution and the extension northwards of the English diet of cheap white bread accompanied by tea, the old oatmeal traditions of porridge, brose and oatcakes were seriously under threat. The fact that they have survived is largely to do with a greater understanding of the nutritional value of oatmeal as its role as a popular 'health' food has become established. Rolled oats, or oatflakes, were developed in America by the Quaker Oat company in 1877: they are made by steaming and rolling pinhead oatmeal. Their introduction greatly eased the process of making porridge and other oatmeal dishes.

There are several water-powered stone-ground mills as well as factory mills kiln-drying and stone-grinding oatmeal in the traditional way.

TECHNIQUE:

The traditional method is first to dry or condition the grain to a moisture content of usually around 15 per cent. It is then spread on a kiln floor, consisting of perforated metal sheets, with a smokeless-fuel furnace some 20–30 feet below. The oats are turned by hand with large shovels until the moisture content is reduced to around 4–5 per cent when the meal has taken on its mild nutty flavour. Milling begins with shelling the husks, then the grains are ground between stones to the required cuts or grades: pinhead (whole grain split into two) – used for haggis; rough – used for porridge, brose and sometimes oatcakes; medium/rough (sometimes known as coarse/medium) – used by butchers for mealie puddings; medium – used for porridge, brose, skirlie and baking; fine and super fine – used in baking and for feeding to babies.

REGION OF PRODUCTION:
SCOTLAND.

Salmon

ADULT SALMON ARE LIKELY TO BE 80CM–1M LONG. WEIGHT: 4–30KG. COLOUR: SILVER ALONG BELLY TURNING TO BLUE-BLACK ALONG BACK, INTERNAL COLOUR VARYING SHADES OF REDDISH-PINK ACCORDING TO FEEDING AND CONDITION.

HISTORY:

Early salmon fisheries on the rivers Tay, Spey, Tweed, Don and Dee produced large catches which were eaten fresh in summer and kippered (smoked and dried) in winter. The quantity caught each year was such that it was one of the most common foods of the people and became so firmly fixed in the minds of the upper classes in Scotland as a cheap, working-man's food that a Highland gentleman, on visiting London, made the mistake of choosing beef for himself and salmon for his servant: 'The Cook, who attended him humoured the Jest, and the Master's eating was Eight Pence and Duncan's came to almost as many Shillings' (Burt, *Letters from the North of Scotland*, 1730).

While supplies of wild salmon remained plentiful for the best part of the last century, there has since been a gradual decline. Over-fishing and netting have been just two of the problems; research is being undertaken to discover the reasons.

Salmon have, of course, been caught in many other rivers as long as they have been prey to Scottish fishermen. There is no simple difference between a Scottish and an English salmon. However, the number and wealth of Scottish streams and their lack of pollution has meant that Scottish Salmon is a regional descriptor of some force and meaning. It has become more distinct and valid with the growth of salmon farming in the last 30 years. As demand for fresh fish increased around the world – and the means to deliver matched the possibilities of sale – so stocks in the wild came under pressure. The expansion of salmon farming, almost exclusively in Scottish waters, was therefore timely. Common standards among producers will allow the existence of rigid quality markers. This is regional food in the making.

Farming began on the West Coast in 1969 and has spread to the Islands, above all the Shetlands, where they market their salmon separately from the rest of Scotland. There have been problems with farmed salmon, but aquaculture has brought employment to a remote and declining population whose traditions have always been based on harvesting from the sea. Many problems have been solved and much research undertaken to farm more efficiently and with less damage to the environment. Skilled farming can produce a high-quality fish which has made its name in the markets of Europe, gaining a French Label Rouge accolade of prime quality.

TECHNIQUE:

During their lifespan salmon go through various stages: in the wild, very young fish, or fry, are at risk from predators and starvation. But after about 3 months in river water, if they survive, they change into parr and then, 1–4 years later, when they are large and strong enough, they change into smolts. They have silvery skins and are, in effect, miniature salmon. Smolts go to sea and feed extensively. Their feeding grounds are thought to be off Greenland and the Faroe Islands. Migration from river and sea generally takes place in early summer, which is another time of high mortality for wild fish.

After only a year at sea, some of the smolts return to the river to spawn; they weigh about 2.25kg, and are known as grilse. The remaining fish stay at sea, growing by about 2.25kg a year. When they return as salmon to fresh water to spawn, it is to their home river where they were hatched. The best quality are caught early in the season when still fat and flavoursome from the rich sea feeding grounds. They are likely to weigh from 8lb to about 60lb. When, and if, they reach their place of hatching and the female spawns and the male ejects his milt on top of the spawn, they become either spent kelts and die from exhaustion and lack of food, or mended kelts and make it back to the sea. Around 5 per cent return to spawn again. They will usually spend 2–3 winters in the sea, sometimes up to 5. The oldest recorded salmon, caught on Loch Maree in Wester Ross, was 13 years old and had spawned 4 times.

Salmon farming depends on breeding stocks which are milked for their eggs in November. The eggs are checked to ensure they are free from disease and they are kept in controlled conditions until they hatch in March. The young fish are very tiny and are carefully monitored. They are reared in special tanks, and as they grow in size are transferred to larger tanks in freshwater lochs, where they grow until they are large enough to be transferred to the sea farms in lochs fed by sea water.

The main practical difference between farmed and wild salmon is that the first is available all year. The debate about the difference in eating quality will long continue. The best farmed fish approach the wild in texture and taste.

REGION OF PRODUCTION:
SCOTLAND.

Food of Scotland

Scotch Pies

DESCRIPTION:

A ROUND, RAISED PIE OF COOKED BEEF OR MUTTON, GENERALLY
9CM DIAMETER, BUT SMALLER ONES (5CM ACROSS) ARE ALSO
MADE. THE HEIGHT IS 3.5–4CM TO THE TOP EDGE, WHICH EX-
TENDS (BY ABOUT 1CM) BEYOND THE ROUND OF PASTRY WHICH
COVERS THE FILLING, MAKING A CENTRAL SPACE FOR HOLDING
'FILLINGS' OR GRAVY. COLOUR: PALE GOLD, THE TOP EDGE USU-
ALLY DARKER GOLD TO DARK BROWN. FLAVOUR: SOMETIMES
QUITE PEPPERY.

HISTORY:

The pie (which is an English word of no certain derivation)
was not indigenous to Scotland. At one critical juncture, it was
identified as a luxurious, immoral introduction from dissolute
England. In 1430, some years after the return of King James I
from exile south of the border, his subjects were upbraided by
the Bishop of St Andrews for their 'wicked usage' and adoption
of the manners of the sophisticated English. The consequence
was a self-denying ordinance – a reduction in the elaboration
of meals in the country at large. Only the gentry, henceforth,
and only on feast days, would be served pies: 'this use of them
not being knowne in Scotland till that season' (Brigid Allen,
Food, 1994).

Scotch pies, once also commonly known as mutton pies, are
descendants of these fifteenth-century villains: a raised pie made
with hot-water paste coaxed up the side of a mould, then left to
set and harden before the filling, is added. It is manufactured in a size
suitable for a single serving. Its popularity appears to have developed
in the latter part of the nineteenth century as industrialization
brought large numbers of people into cities, where wages were low
and living (and cooking) conditions poor. Made by local bakers,
itinerant pie-men or -women or by tavern cooks, the 'hot-pie'
('het-pey' in Dundee) became a sustaining convenience food for

workers. They had to be eaten hot: either hot from the bakers, or reheated at home. Some bakers who provided the 'hot-pie' service also kept a jug of hot gravy for pouring into the centre of the pie. Tinned beans and mashed potatoes became popular 'fillers' piled up in the space above the meat.

At first, the pie was always minced mutton, making use of tough, mature meat unsuitable for other purposes. This has largely been superseded today by beef. McNeill (1929) quotes a St Andrews professor describing the pies of his childhood which were made by the pie-wife: 'Delightful as were her pigeon and apple pies, her chef-d'oeuvre … was a certain kind of mutton-pie. The mutton was minced to the smallest consistency, and was made up in standing crust, which was strong enough to contain the most delicious gravy … There were no lumps of fat or grease in them at all … They always arrived piping hot … It makes my mouth water still when I think of those pies.'

On the West Coast, the most renowned pie-maker was also a woman, known as 'Granny Black', whose tavern in the Candleriggs in Glasgow became Mecca for pie-lovers around the early 1900s.

Though sold today from all bakeries on a daily basis, the hot-pie trade moves into mass-production on Saturdays as they are delivered to football grounds for eating at half-time – with a cup of hot Bovril. An average-sized baker's, with a football ground to supply on a Saturday, could make 35,000 pies each week.

Smaller, half-size pies are made by a few bakers. The range of fillings has now extended beyond plain and simple minced beef. Some are made with onion; others are still filled with mutton as of old; some have chopped beef steak rather than mince, when they are described as steak pies; more adventurous concoctions may be suitable for vegetarians, perhaps a custard of cheese and tomato, macaroni cheese, or vegetables in a savoury custard. These last are mostly baked without the pastry lids.

TECHNIQUE:

A hot-water paste is made, but using beef dripping instead of the lard – rendered pig fat – used in England. The proportion of flour to fat is relatively high, about 4:1; this is shaped in the pie-moulding machine before it cools. The pie shells are left overnight to harden. The meat is prepared and seasoned with salt, pepper and other spices such as mace or nutmeg; this is used to fill the cases about half-full. The lids are placed on top and the pies baked in a very hot oven for 15–20 minutes.

REGION OF PRODUCTION:
SCOTLAND.

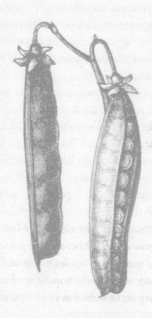

Tablet

DESCRIPTION:

SUGAR CANDY IN OBLONG BLOCKS 15–20MM THICK, MARKED INTO 30MM SQUARES. COLOUR: PALE TO DARK BROWN. FLAVOUR AND TEXTURE: VERY SWEET; CRISP BUT MELTING. COMPOSITION: SUGAR, THIN CREAM OR MILK, SOMETIMES BUTTER. VARIANTS MAY CONTAIN CINNAMON, COCONUT, GINGER, LEMON, ORANGE, PEPPERMINT, VANILLA, WALNUT, CHOCOLATE.

HISTORY:

First used as a sweet vehicle for sour medicines, medicinal tablets were made by apothecaries in both England and Scotland. The term was abandoned in England but continued in Scotland, transferring to an item of confectionery as sugar from the West Indies became plentiful in the nineteenth century. Scotland has much distinctive confectionery but tablet has arguably the longest history. Certainly it is now the most widely made, with national rather than regional repute. Early documentation is in the household book of Lady Grisell Baillie (1692–1733) referring to 'taiblet for the bairns'.

While Grisell Baillie was buying tablet for her children, Mrs McLintock, author of the first published Scottish cookery book, was writing recipes for 'tablets' (*Mrs McLintock's Receipts for Cookery and Pastry Work*, 1736). To make Orange Tablets with the Grate [zest]; To make Rose Tablets; To make Ginger Tablets; and To make Cinnamon Tablets: 'Take half an ounce of cinnamon, beat and search [sieve] it, or take four Guts [drops] of the Spirit of Cinnamon [distilled bruised cinnamon and rose water] to a pound of sugar; take half a mutchkin of water, clarify it with the white of an egg, put it on a slow fire, and boil it till it be almost candy'd and put in the four Guts of the Spirit of Cinnamon, mix them well together, rub the papers wither with sweet oil or fresh butter and pour it out, and cut them in small four corner's pieces.'

Today tablet is distinguished from fudge by its crisp bite. The degree of bite depends on the richness of the ingredients. Tablet has less butter and glucose than fudge; it is also boiled to a slightly lower temperature.

TECHNIQUE:

Sugar, water, single cream and/or milk (sometimes condensed milk), butter (commercial makers also add glucose and/or fondant while some domestic recipes suggest syrup or vinegar) are boiled to 115°C (soft ball). While still hot, the mixture is beaten until it begins to grain slightly. It is poured into a buttered tray and left until just set before marking into small squares.

REGION OF PRODUCTION:
SCOTLAND.

Tayberry, Tummelberry

DESCRIPTION:

TAYBERRY: A LONG FRUIT (ABOUT 4CM), DEEP PURPLE-RED WHEN FULLY RIPE, WITH A SWEET AND AROMATIC FLAVOUR. TUMMELBERRY: DEEPER RED WITH A SLIGHTLY ROUNDER FRUIT AND SHARPER, LESS AROMATIC FLAVOUR.

HISTORY:

Tayberries and Tummelberries (named for rivers whose valleys disgorge on the Strathmore area, the main berry-producing region of eastern Scotland) are derived from a long tradition of fruit cross-breeding which began in America in the 1860s with Judge Logan's berry when he set about crossing a cultivated (and too bland for his liking) blackberry with a wild variety with more flavour.

The Tayberry is a hybrid of an unnamed raspberry bred at the Scottish Crop Research Institute at Invergowrie (1978) and the blackberry cultivar Aurora from Oregon. The Tummelberry is a newer hybrid, obtained by crossing the Tayberry with one of its sister hybrids (1984). The Scottish contribution, particularly the Tayberry, is now grown widely in the USA as a commercial crop with a plant patent, also in France, Germany, Holland and Scandinavia, while at home it has established itself most successfully on farms which have a pick-your-own facility.

TECHNIQUE:

Tayberries and Tummelberries are commercially cultivated in the open, on a post and wire support system. Like blackberries, they grow best in well-drained, medium loam with a pH of about 6.5 and do best on sites with a sheltered, sunny aspect.

REGION OF PRODUCTION:

SOUTH SCOTLAND AND GENERAL SCOTLAND.